PARENTING YOUR ADULT CHILD

PARENTING YOUR ADULT CHILD

KEEPING THE FAITH
(AND YOUR SANITY)

SUSAN V. VOGT

ST. ANTHONY MESSENGER PRESS
Cincinnati, Ohio

Scripture passages have been taken from *New Revised Standard Version Bible,* copyright ©1989 by the Division of Christian Education of the National Council of the Churches of Christ in the U.S.A., and used by permission. All rights reserved.

Cover and book design by Mark Sullivan
Cover image © Ocean Photography | Veer

LIBRARY OF CONGRESS CATALOGING-IN-PUBLICATION DATA
Vogt, Susan.
Parenting your adult child : keeping the faith (and your sanity) / Susan Vogt.
p. cm.
Includes bibliographical references (p.   ).
ISBN 978-0-86716-972-0 (pbk. : alk. paper) 1. Parenting--Religious aspects--Catholic Church. 2. Parent and adult child--Religious aspects--Catholic Church. I. Title.
BX2352.V64 2011
248.8′45--dc22
2010040901

ISBN 978-0-86716-972-0

Copyright © 2011, Susan V. Vogt. All rights reserved.

Published by St. Anthony Messenger Press
28 W. Liberty St.
Cincinnati, OH 45202
www.AmericanCatholic.org
www.SAMPBooks.org

Printed in the United States of America.

Printed on acid-free paper.

11 12 13 14 15   5 4 3 2 1

To my own young adults–Brian, Heidi, Dacian, and Aaron Vogt–
who trained me well and gave me permission to open their lives to
the world.

To two dear friends who died during the writing of this book and
whose deaths are a great loss to me and to our human community
still struggling here on earth–Jim McGinnis, cofounder with his
wife, Kathy, of Parenting for Peace and Justice and the Institute for
Peace and Justice, and Father Mark Schmieder, member of the
Anawim Community, prison chaplain, and advocate for the poor and
disenfranchised in Greater Cincinnati.

Contents

Saying goodbye to your children as they set off to find their way in the world feels like creating a Picasso or Michelangelo and then giving it away. It's almost like missing a limb or an organ. You must dwell on their successes and not their absence. You must celebrate their achievements and not wallow in missing them.

–Anonymous parent

PREFACE

THOSE READING THIS BOOK DESERVE to know where I place my own faith. I am a practicing Roman Catholic who wants very much for our church to live up to the daunting challenge of faith given us by Jesus Christ. For many years, I worked professionally for the Catholic church as codirector (with my husband, Jim) of family ministry for the Diocese of Covington, Kentucky, and prior to that in Kalamazoo, Michigan. I am still a committed Catholic and do freelance speaking and writing on the themes of marriage, parenting, and spirituality. Because of my own faith tradition, much of this book is grounded in examples from the Catholic experience of faith.

But, because I believe that God is bigger than any one faith tradition, I think readers will find that both young adults' search for the meaning of life and the angst that some parents feel about their young adults' "lack of faith" transcend religious affiliation. The same principles apply whether a person is a faithful Catholic parent steeped in church tradition or any other devoted religious parent concerned about the secularization of their children.

Likewise, those who seek meaning, inspiration, and spirituality in their lives will find common ingredients to their journey regardless of their starting place. Authentic wisdom is usually transferable from Catholic to Protestant, from Jew to Muslim, from Quaker to Unitarian, from Hindu to Buddhist, or from secular humanist to seekers uncertain about where to place their hearts and souls. My belief is that there is a God who created the universe and who loves us all unconditionally. The rest is history.

Because I have walked in your parental shoes, I invite you to explore with me how to respect and nurture the faith that lies deep within each of our young adults, no matter what it looks like on the surface. The spiritual challenges that you face as an elder are not only for the benefit of your child but will require honed virtues and deeper faith on your own part. As you negotiate bumps along the road of later parenthood, be consoled by the knowledge that many have gone before us, and we can learn from their successes and mistakes.

In creating this parenting resource for you, I have collected insights from a broad range of young adults and their parents and have sorted these insights into what helped, what seemed counterproductive, and what was, to be honest, a waste of time and breath. May my work save you some anxiety, give you some helpful strategies, and bring you greater peace of mind.

Susan V. Vogt

How to Read This Book

As you can see from the table of contents, chapters are listed according to typical young adult life transitions. There is no big mystery here. Read the chapters that apply to the life transition that concerns you.

You'll note I've included fifteen virtues for parents plus prayer. While certain virtues pertain to some stages more than others, you will no doubt need to call on all of these virtues while parenting your grown children. You may find yourself skipping ahead or revisiting key virtues as your needs warrant. That is to be expected. Our spiritual lives don't operate in straight lines that neatly follow chronological age–but the virtues remain constant throughout.

Another aspect of your young adult's transitions is your *own* transition. So I also ask: What challenges do you, the parent, face as a result? Families are a system. When one person changes, everyone in the family is affected by that change. Although it may be distressing at times to watch your young adult struggle or ignore you, consider these times to be opportunities when God calls you to a deeper faith and trust. Just as your child is growing and changing, so are you. Embrace these transitions, for, as speaker and author Matthew Kelly often emphasizes, the process will "help you become the best version of yourself."

I encourage you to use this book as a form of spiritual direction or your own personalized retreat. Reflecting on the Scripture connected with each parental virtue and the reflection questions that end each chapter can help you do this. Pause occasionally to ponder how the insights you're gaining and the Word of God is calling you to a more mature faith. Additionally, throughout the book, you will notice "Thoughts to Keep In Mind," which will reinforce thoughts, themes, and ideas discussed in each chapter.

Some may find it supportive to read this book with a group of friends. The reflection questions can serve as a do-it-yourself faith-sharing guide.

Finally, there are two appendices: one that includes results of the survey I conducted to help with my research for this book and another that offers a prayer service and ritual for when an adult child leaves home.

Introduction

IT'S EIGHTEEN YEARS AFTER THE birth of your child. How did your baby grow up so quickly? As a parent, do you have anything left to say to your young adult? Is there anything your child still needs to hear from you—or will tolerate your saying? When you first held your baby in your arms and realized that you had an awesome responsibility to guide and protect this child for the next eighteen years, it probably felt daunting. Now that your child has become an adult, you may feel just as frightened to let go. Or, you may ask, should I ever completely let go?

While your legal and financial responsibility for your offspring may be waning (I know, this may sound ludicrous to a parent facing college tuition payments, but those, too, shall pass), the emotional nurturing of your child will continue indefinitely as you encounter thorny parenting issues such as:

- When to rescue and when to allow your adult child to falter
- When to push and when to restrain yourself
- How to assist your young adult in life decisions without taking over
- How to keep your faith when your child seems to be abandoning it
- How to forgive yourself for the mistakes you made in parenting along the way
- How to move into an adult relationship with this amazing person you have raised

As a parent of four young adults, I have faced and been challenged by these issues—and more. I have listened carefully to other parents, learned a lot, and come to know that we parents of adult children need all the support, guidance, and consolation we can get. In short, how do we relate to our adult children and still keep our sanity, our faith, and our love?

CREATING A MORE SOPHISTICATED RELATIONSHIP WITH YOUR CHILD

Just as your child has matured in wisdom and grace during the past eighteen-plus years—and pulled you along into becoming a wiser, more mature person along the way—so now your parent-child relationship is becoming more sophisticated. Sometimes you may find the tables turned as you, the parent, become the learner and receiver of assistance. Sometimes you may doubt yourself and your ability. Always, however, you remain a parent.

These young adults whom we love cover a broad spectrum when it comes to spirituality and faith. The refrain I hear often from parents is, "I'm proud of my young adults. They are loving, generous people who care about making this world a better place, *but* they no longer go to church." Many parents find this a distressing situation; others feel resigned to it; still others put the future in God's hands and pray a lot.

Which of the following scenarios fits the young adults in your family? They:

- have never strayed from the faith of their youth and seem to be doing quite well
- have discovered faith in a new and intense way despite the perhaps laissez-faire commitment of your own faith practices. In fact, they may follow their faith more strictly than you do.
- may not be quite sure how they feel about organized religion. They are seeking meaning and purpose to their lives and trying to sort out the best path.

- have drifted from faith practices. They may be "Chreaster Christians" (Christmas/Easter churchgoers) who have not found anything to keep them connected to church other than family loyalty.
- may be angry at the church for real or perceived short-comings, such as clergy sexual abuse of children, lack of compassion at an important life transition (birth, marriage, death), or disagreement with church doctrine on issues such as ordination, family planning, or homosexuality

THERE IS FAITH AND THERE IS FAITH

Finding faith is bigger than organized religion, but the practice of a specific religion is often where young adults and their parents experience tension. In this book we'll look at both "open faith" (which transcends religions) and "focused faith" (which includes commitment in a specific faith tradition).

What do we mean by the word *faith*? *Faith* is such a short, seemingly simple word, but it can mean many things, depending on how broadly we define it. For most people, *faith* has a specifically religious meaning, but it can also be broadened to faith in self, family, or the values one believes in. For example, faith can be:

1. A belief in and practice of a specific organized religion
2. A belief in a religion even though one does not regularly attend worship services or abide by all its teachings
3. A general belief that there is a God (or some higher power for which humans have created various names) and there is life after death
4. A belief in the spiritual nature of humankind—that we are not on earth just for our own pleasure but to make a positive difference in the world and contribute to the common good
5. A generalized belief in positive values such as honesty, generosity, thoughtfulness, a respect for life, loyalty to family, and a commitment to be true to these values

6. A cultural obligation to worship God in a specific way even though it has no direct personal meaning

In a separate category, I put the evangelical sense of faith, which asks the question, "Do you accept Jesus as your Lord and Savior?" Under this definition of faith, someone who is not a public, professed Christian cannot be saved. This presents the dilemma of how to regard the many fine and upstanding people in the world (many of whom are young adults) who do not publicly profess Jesus. Can they be saved? I leave that answer to those who are still counting the number of angels that can dance on the head of a pin.

For our purposes, I consider the first five descriptions of faith to be authentic. Nominal or cultural faith (number six) is a duty that does not deserve the title *faith*; it is simply going through religious motions and is a charade. Of course, loyalty to family can often undergird the rote exercise of religious rituals, and that bumps up the definition to at least number five. Most important, my belief is that God can work in any situation, even touching those who have no explicit faith.

Losing One's Faith

We may "lose" our glasses, car keys, or a computer file, but most of the time we know that the missing object resides somewhere. (Well, maybe that computer document really is gone forever.) Hopefully, we eventually find what was lost, since it still exists; it just wasn't visible to us. Faith can be like that. It may go "underground" for a while–sometimes for a long while, eventually to resurface in a different, more significant form. It's not really gone; we just don't know how to recognize it.

Virtue's Role in Faith

Generally speaking, *virtue* refers to right living or good habits. Traditionally, virtues have been categorized into:

- Theological Virtues–faith, hope, and love
- Cardinal Virtues–prudence (wisdom), temperance (restraint), courage (fortitude), and justice
- Seven Gifts of the Spirit–wisdom, awe in the presence of the Lord, fortitude, reverence, understanding, counsel, and knowledge (Isaiah 11:2-5)
- Fruits of the Spirit–love, joy, peace, patience, kindness, goodness, trustfulness, gentleness, self-control, goodness, generosity (Galatians 5:22 and 2 Peter 1:5-7)
- Beatitudes–spirit of poverty, gentleness, compassion, justice, mercy, purity of heart, peacemaking (Matthew 5:3-12)

For the purposes of this book, I've drawn from these classic virtues and added contemporary virtues that I believe are good habits to develop as a parent transitions from the role of caretaker to a guide by the side of an adult child. The virtues I've identified are not the only ones that can help parents deepen their own spirituality, but they are especially relevant to forming new relationships with those we love.

LISTENING TO OTHER VOICES

Many of the insights in this book are based on results of my national survey, to which more than six hundred people responded. These voices, combined with those of colleagues and the many parents I listen to while giving talks around the country, informed my thinking and writing. (See Appendix A for an overview of the survey and statistics.) Although some advice here is a result of my own ruminations about how to influence young adults in faith, most comes from the experience of these other parents, who were willing to share what they learned from their successes and mistakes. Wisdom doesn't always come from doing it right; it often comes from reflecting on what went wrong and how to fix it. All of this is tested by matching it up with the perceptions of young adults themselves–what they found moved them toward a belief in God and what got in their way. (Sometimes it was the parents who were the stumbling block.).

Although not everyone surveyed agreed on how to keep faith alive (or find it for the first time) after a young adult leaves home, I found some common threads that ran through each generation's responses:

1. Young adults generally admired their parents for being hard-working, stable, and committed. This often took the form of commitment to their faith and to lifelong marriage. Young adults yearned for the comfort of tradition.

2. While some Generation X- and Y-ers take a sabbatical from organized religion, others seem to crave reverence, solemnity, structure, and authority in their spiritual search. This may seem strange to parents who rebelled against the formality, strict enforcement of rules, and rote prayers of the 1960s to 1980s. Having been raised in a time of less-structured catechesis, however, twenty- and thirty-somethings often didn't have as solid a foundation in church teaching. Sometimes morality was presented to them as very relative, and that made it hard to be sure of moral choices. In a complex, changing world, many young adults want something certain to guide their lives. As one religious educator, Margaret Davis of St. Petersburg, Florida, put it on her survey, "They came of age when religious education was too often comprised of 'God is love. Now make a collage to reflect this.'"

3. Young adults often criticized their parents for complacently going along with the crowd, doing what's expected, and believing because they were raised to obey without question. In other words, many young adults thought their parents were a bunch of followers.

4. Parents admired the willingness of young adults to explore, be flexible, and volunteer. They also saw young adults as having an inquisitive attitude, an optimism for life, and individualism. Often

parents pointed to a young adult's much stronger commitment to work for social justice, particularly environmental causes. One parent shared a story of her college-aged son's selflessness and compassion: When he saw that his mother was having difficulty cleaning up after an incontinent older relative, he insisted on doing it for her.

5. Parents, however, found enough to criticize in their young adults, too. Often criticism centered around experimentation and lack of commitment. One parent's comments summed it up: "They flit from cause to cause, job to job, and worse, from person to person. Continuity is missing."

6. Many parents advised against force-feeding faith and preaching about religion to young adults. "Let go and let God," was a common refrain. This was often followed by, "Pray, pray, pray."

7. As hard as it is to watch a rebellious or apathetic young adult walk away from a faith the parent holds dear, many parents were wise enough to realize that sometimes you must lose faith to find it. In other words, sometimes the "faith" these children practiced when they were younger was an inherited faith. These young adults may not really own it until they walk away and reflect on what is missing in their lives. In time, this may prompt them to claim faith for themselves. It reminds me of the adage, "If you love someone, set her free, if she comes back, it's meant to be."

8. Probably the hardest-won counsel from parents was to honor the mysterious ways of God. It's natural for parents to want to rescue their children from mistakes, pain, and even tragedy. But time after time, parents and their young adults told bittersweet stories of how it was only by falling flat on their faces that these young adults felt the most need for God. Sometimes it was in the emptiness of not knowing where to turn that God entered their lives.

In sum, it is the parents' job to keep loving their children, no matter what; and it is the young adults' job to keep seeking, no matter what.

Faith is a decision that each person must make for herself, but community is what sustains faith. The rest of this book explores this dynamic and how to foster it.

I did encounter some surprises from my research and survey. A few responses were pretty implausible. For example, although all parents found at least some qualities to admire in their young adults, several young adults found *absolutely nothing* that they admired about the older generation (and said so defiantly). On the other hand, one parent said *all* of her children "were godly adults; none of them were difficult; were *never* at odds about faith; and all of them attend Mass every week without exception." While I am sure she may feel this way and believe this to be true, the likelihood of her experience (true or not) resembling others' is not likely.

I also found it interesting that many parents said they have become personal friends with St. Monica and now bombard her with petitions. They found comfort in her devotion to God and her incessant praying for her son, Augustine, the once-sinner turned devoutly religious man and eventual saint.

Although conventional wisdom characterizes parents as old fuddy-duddies who have difficulty making changes or trying something new, I was surprised by how many young adults fretted that their parents were "too flexible" about their own faith. This often came from neoconservatives who were too young to remember the strict and elaborate rules of pre–Vatican II Catholicism. These young adults liked the clarity and surety of knowing exactly what was right and the feeling of being rooted in a religion that had a two-thousand-year history. It's a real role reversal.

WHY BOTHER WITH FAITH?
This may seem an odd question to ask in a book that presumes the value of faith, not only in the broad sense of seeking spiritual meaning but also in the narrower sense of commitment to a specific faith.

A compelling reason, I think, is that it gives us, young and old, a reason to get up in the morning. Why? Because it's all about loving beyond what is reasonable.

Think of it this way: For many adults, the reason we get up in the morning is love. It may be love for our work or a cause to which we're committed. Even more often, it may be love for another human being with whom we share our lives. For many people, love for our children who need us gives us a reason to face another day. Sprinkle this with days when we get up anticipating a special treat–a trip, a birthday, a visit to an amusement park, or simply the anticipation of the unknown–and many things move us from prone to standing.

Eventually, however, there come times when life looks bleak or boring, when we may not have a specific love that prompts us to get up in the morning. Perhaps it's a time of crisis or tragedy. Perhaps the nest is empty or retirement has lost its freshness. With nothing delightful to look forward to, some ask, "Is this all there is to life?"

That's when we must dig deep and ask those questions about the meaning of our lives. For the secularist, there may be no reason left, especially if he's experiencing pain or sadness in life. For a person of faith, however, each day offers another opportunity to love people and creation and to contribute to making this world a better place.

Because it has to do with the ultimate meaning of life, faith gives us a reason to get up in the morning.

All this talk about finding the meaning of life and faith can sound pretty fuzzy and esoteric. Does this mean faith is just a matter of being a good person? Where does God come into all of it? Of course, for religious people, God is the Creator, Savior, and Sustainer of Life. But *where is* this invisible presence we call God? I like to think of it as looking for Waldo in the classic children's book, *Where's Waldo?* Waldo is on every page, mixed in with hordes of humans, but we have to look at all the different people to find him. He's not usually obvious, but he's always there, hidden among a lot of people.

One of the great insights of the Catholic faith is that we not only believe that God is present in our neighbors and all of creation, but we also have the very physical and intimate experience of God becoming one with us through the Eucharist. Jesus must have known that human motivation and inspiration weaken over time, and thus he gave us a way to remember him. It's possible to be spiritual and remember the presence of God without this, but, being human, we tend to forget.

: THOUGHTS TO KEEP IN MIND :

Pray, pray, pray.

It is your job to keep loving your child, no matter what.
It is your child's job to keep seeking, no matter what.

When one person changes, the change impacts
everyone in the family.

Fifteen Virtues (plus Prayer) for Parents of Grown Children

A NUMBER OF THE VIRTUES in this book have their roots in the spirituality of the Society of Mary (Marianists), which outlines a path to holiness called the "System of Virtues." I have drawn from this heritage but given many of the virtues more contemporary titles. Although each virtue can stand alone, they also build on one another.

Virtues are deliberate efforts to develop positive, healthy, God-centered ways of thinking and behaving. Cultivating these virtues will help you assist your young adult with making decisions without taking over.

The Virtue of Silence of Words

> When words are many,
>   transgression is not lacking,
> but the prudent are restrained in speech. (Proverbs 10:19)

"Silence of words" may sound like a strange name for a virtue and not one most people are familiar with. The gist of it is that we must discipline our mouth so that what comes out of it furthers the work of God and does not interfere with it. I often call this "mindfulness of words," since it doesn't mean that we're always silent but rather that we choose our words carefully. In the case of parents of young adults, however, the challenge is often to make significant adjustments in our pattern of talking–for example, to stop nagging and start biting our tongue.

This requires a tremendous amount of self-control, and I myself have been working on this virtue for almost forty years. (I think I'm getting better. My kids wonder, but they don't have the perspective of time and knowing how much less I am saying than I could.) Following are some dimensions of silence of words to consider.

Talk shorter. One thing I've learned about speaking and writing is that shorter messages usually have a stronger impact than longer ones. (My children were my primary teachers of this maxim–the longer I spoke, the less they listened.) If "talking short" comes easily to you, be grateful, and check yourself to make sure you are sharing enough of yourself with your young adult and not just letting this fall to the other parent. If you're like many parents and believe that there is so much information, caution, and wisdom you want to pour into your young adult–and so little time–don't just talk faster and louder. STOP. Stop and think before you launch into sharing your unsolicited opinions and beliefs. Talking shorter also allows you to listen more. Ask yourself the following:

- Have I said this before?
- If it didn't make a difference then, what makes me think repeating it will change things?
- Can she get the same message from my actions without my having to put it into words?
- Is there a creative, new way I can convey this message?
- Is there a way humor can make the point?
- Is there someone else who can convey this message in a fresher way?

Talk smarter. When you work at talking shorter, it becomes incumbent upon you to make your words count. Although small talk about the weather and the neighbors has its place, don't let small talk dominate your limited conversation time. On the other hand, too much heavy talk can be deadening. This is why the wise parent needs to think ahead about how to craft a message that hits important points without too many words. This takes effort, and you as the parent must hone your skills as a communicator and not let conversations slide into repetitive jargon. To talk smarter, you must really think through your positions, sometimes do background reading, and not spout opinions based solely on popular notions or personal biases.

If you don't feel verbally articulate–or even if you do–sometimes the most effective way to communicate a message is to use an alternate medium. Watching movies, listening to songs, or sharing experiences of wonder together can often touch the spirit more convincingly than the most well-chosen words. Be cautious, however, of being too heavy-handed or "in your face" about movies or music. Do things together, talk about them, listen to your child's perspective. Ask thought-provoking questions. Subtlety is often better than preaching. Your child is now an adult. He will get it–eventually, after it rolls around in his subconscious a while.

Put it in writing. Writing helps you hone your words to the basic message and censor anything that smacks of paternalism, criticism, or judgment. Letters by snail mail can be effective since they are so rare these days. But don't underestimate a well-timed and meaningful e-mail, too. Instant messages, text messages, and Facebook statuses also seem to get a child's attention, and with the fewest number of words! A quick "Remember I love you" note may seem trite, but it could reach your child at the moment she needs it most.

Share your faith struggles, not just your certainty. The one thing that you definitely should put into words are your own stories of faith, especially any struggles you've faced. Sharing your experiences of doubt, frustration, or vulnerability in seeking God not only are more interesting, they put a human face on faith and open the door to young adults' sharing their own struggles. Carefully pick a time without distractions–perhaps during a long car ride or late at night. Young adults seem programmed to discuss life's ultimate questions late at night, over a glass of something or other.

Take time for silence. The virtue of silence is not just about talking less or smarter, it is also about taking the time at this stage in your life to be alone in silence. Quiet time may last just a moment or two if you have other children at home vying for your attention, but don't neglect the need for contemplation whenever you feel stressed. In the midst of his healing and preaching, Jesus periodically took time to be away by himself and pray. It's not that Jesus didn't have important things to do and people clamoring for his help, but he must have recognized the value of reconnecting with his Father in a very direct and private way. Jesus went off by himself to pray. We should too. Be sure to pass this wisdom to your children (best if done by example), emphasizing the importance of quiet time, solitude, and the need to get away to refresh.

Trust your lifetime of actions. The religious counterpart to "Actions speak louder than words" is St. Francis of Assisi's saying, "Preach the Gospel at all times. If necessary, use words."

2. THE VIRTUE OF IMAGINATION

> Then the disciples came and asked him, "Why do you speak to them in parables?" He answered,... "The reason I speak to them in parables is that 'seeing they do not perceive, and hearing they do not listen, nor do they understand.'" (Matthew 13:10, 13)

> Just then some men came, carrying a paralyzed man on a bed. They were trying to bring him in and lay him before Jesus; but finding no way to bring him in because of the crowd, they went up on the roof and let him down with his bed through the tiles into the middle of the crowd in front of Jesus. (Luke 5:18-19)

Routines are good, but. . . The virtue of imagination goes beyond your relationship with your young adult. By having experienced a good amount of life, it's natural to have developed habits, routines, and certain ways of thinking. Most of these are useful to daily life. You probably have developed eating, sleeping, and health-care routines. Most likely you have ways to remember birthdays, a system for handling your finances, and certain ways and times that you pray. These all help you stay faithful to important commitments.

Routines, however, can become ruts. To stay alive physically, mentally, and spiritually, it's helpful at times to mix it up. Maybe you've always had meat and potatoes for dinner, and so far you feel fine. It might be healthier, however, for you to experiment with a broader variety of menus. You may have always read the daily paper, but it may stretch your mind to see what news is available on public radio or the Internet.

Force-feed yourself ideas. Try asking yourself the same question five times and forcing yourself to come up with a different answer each time—no matter how crazy. For example, "How can I get my young adult to go to church while at college?" Answer #1: I can ask or tell him to go. Answer #2: I can remind him with a weekly e-mail. Answer #3: I can bribe him with money. Answer #4: I can try the "Fantastiks" approach and tell him that the one thing I *don't* want him to do is go to church on Sunday. Answer #5: I can find a really hot girl who goes to church and orchestrate a "chance" meeting. Whoops. This question might require at least ten answers, and you might just end up with Answer #99: I can let go, and let God.

Stretch yourself and experiment. Most importantly, you may have developed a pattern about how you pray, and it may feel comfortable. It can also become mindless, as you repeat words automatically without focusing on what you are saying. For example, have you ever had the experience of saying a memorized prayer so automatically that when you finish, you realize that you had little consciousness of what you were saying? You just moved your lips and put in your time? I have. How do you get beyond these good but limited habits? The answer is similar to furthering your physical or mental health: Mix it up. Use your imagination to experiment with different kinds of prayer. Perhaps it's time to consult a spiritual advisor to help you deepen your prayer or find different styles of prayer. Maybe it's time to imagine God through different images than you used as a child or young adult. Talk, read, experiment. You're not dead yet!

3. THE VIRTUE OF RESTRAINT

> For this very reason, you must make every effort to support your faith with goodness, and goodness with knowledge, and knowledge with self-control, and self-control with endurance, and endurance with godliness, and godliness with mutual affection, and mutual affection with love. (2 Peter 1:5-7)

> By contrast, the fruit of the Spirit is love, joy, peace, patience, kindness, generosity, faithfulness, gentleness, and self-control. (Galatians 5:22)

The virtue that undergirds both silence of words and imagination is restraint: the ability to be patient. It's a heroic virtue because it requires you to exercise extreme self-control while allowing your young adult to make her own mistakes. You thought it was hard to let your child miss the elementary school bus because she fussed about what clothes to wear. You may have agonized over her less-than-energetic preparation for the SAT or ACT. These experiences have been preparation for letting your daughter pay an exorbitant non-sufficient-funds fee on her bank account or finding that her professor doesn't consider "I was up all night vomiting" a valid excuse for missing the final exam. (Don't ask how I know these things.)

Wait. Developing patience and restraint is necessary. It says that not everything has to be done in *my* time and in *my* way. It's another way to turn our lives and worries over to the wisdom of God. We wait because it does not all depend on us. We wait because we trust in God's timing. We wait because it can take time to let faith grow.

Ponder. Look back on your own life and ponder how you came to faith–not so much the inherited practices of faith or learning the teachings of the church but rather a deeper, more personally felt faith. Have there been times when you felt the powerful presence of God, or has it been more like the "tiny whispering sound" that Elijah recognizes as the Lord passing by (1 Kings 19:13)? The more you deepen an awareness of God's presence and ways in your own life, the more you'll be able to let God work in the lives of others without trying to control God. If you can't think of times when God has directly or subtly been present to you, then maybe that's the place to start. Seek a more personal relationship with this God whom you want your young adult to love too.

Train your body to help. If you're having trouble cultivating the virtue of restraint, try the Alcoholics Anonymous tenet of accepting the things you have no power to change. You might try using the natural breathing rhythm of your body to remind yourself of your goal of patience. It goes like this: As you take a breath in, think *acceptance*. As you exhale, think *surrender*. Repeat. Accept your child and your own humanity. Surrender to God who loves you and your young adult more than you can ever imagine. This practice, or other self-talk like it, helps us detach from our young adults. Yes, they'll always be our children, we'll always love them and welcome them home, but we're no longer responsible for them.

4. The Virtue of Ingenuity

> "See, I am sending you out like sheep into the midst of wolves; so be wise as serpents and innocent as doves." (Matthew 10:16)

The virtue of ingenuity is most needed when dealing with young adults, because they've known you long enough to have heard all of your beliefs and arguments more than once. Although you've been a respected person of influence in their lives, repeating your message in the same way is still called nagging. You must take the time and ingenuity to find creative and interesting ways to converse with them as adults. Think before you speak: Is there a different way to say what is on your mind? Does it sound at all critical or judgmental?

Don't be a "Johnny One Note." If you must leave articles strategically lying around the house or forward inspirational e-mails, send wisdom of all sorts, not just religious pieces. The more predictable and repetitive a parent's message is, the deafer the young adult (or anyone) becomes to the message.

Be indirect. Instead of directly bringing up issues of religious practice, consider engaging your child in conversations that border on religion, such as ethics or a current moral issue. Talk about the larger spiritual context and how different moral actions impact the individual and the common good. Place the church's position within the larger framework of spirituality.

5. THE VIRTUE OF MINDFULNESS OF EMOTIONS

> Therefore do not worry, saying, "What will we eat?" or "What will we drink?" or "What will we wear?" For it is the Gentiles who strive for all these things; and indeed your heavenly Father knows that you need all these things. But strive first for the kingdom of God and his righteousness, and all these things will be given to you as well. "So do not worry about tomorrow, for tomorrow will bring worries of its own. Today's trouble is enough for today." (Matthew 6:31-34)

Perhaps the most challenging virtue to cultivate during your young adult's twenties is not to let your emotions run away with you. Emotions are good. They fill our hearts with joy, alert us to problems, and, when necessary, stir us to action. They also can muck up the thinking side of our being and cause undue stress and angst. Since the positive emotions of joy, gratitude, happiness, and so forth do not usually cause parents concern, we will focus on the trouble-some ones: worry, sadness, disappointment, fear, and anger.

Worry. Worry is endemic to parenting. We worry because we care. Although worries about childhood illnesses, grades, and who is whose best friend are history, they're replaced with bigger concerns, such as, "Will my son find a meaningful job or a soul mate or get off drugs or out of debt?" When dealing with worries, the first step is to discern whether you have a "productive" worry. In other words, will your worrying change or prevent anything? Usually the answer is no. That doesn't mean, however, that the worry will disappear.

If you've determined that your worry is unproductive but you can't get rid of it, substitute a positive thought, pray, and throw yourself into service to others. Look for someone to care for who is in worse shape than you are. Your own worries may pale. If the worry warrants action, tell your young adult your worry–once. Provide information, if it would be helpful and well received, and then take up that service project. If you need a mantra, try my personal favorite: "Martha, Martha, you are worried and distracted by many things; there is need of only one thing" (Luke 10:41). Then be present to your young adult when you're together, but don't dwell on the worry.

Sadness. It's natural for parents to feel sad when something unfortunate happens to their child. Your daughter didn't get the job she had her heart set on. Her boyfriend broke up with her. You empathize with your young adult, hold her in prayer, and probably go on with life. Sadness can also come from inaction. You hoped that she would become involved with the same faith that you hold dear, but she hasn't. You know, however, that she's a good person with strong values, and you trust God will be with her. You continue to hold her in prayer, are attentive to whether there are times when she wants to talk and go on.

Disappointment. Disappointment is a little stronger than sadness, but not much. Your child may have decided to live with his girlfriend. He may have chosen a lifestyle of conspicuous consumption. Both situations may be contrary to your values, but your response to disappointment usually should be to wait. Give advice if it's requested. You can carefully, creatively, and tentatively offer information if he seems receptive to it. Combat disappointment primarily with prayer and time. If you find yourself unduly wallowing in disappointment, you might try one of the following:

- Reserve judgment on what you perceive to be negative behavior. It is God's place to judge, not ours. There may be circumstances of which you're unaware that mitigate your young adult's actions, but you don't know everything. So wait. Things may change.
- Remind yourself that you, too, have disappointed others at some time in your life. (I'm sure you have, haven't you?)
- Remind yourself of one or more of your young adult's positive qualities that make you proud.
- Turn your young adult over to God again.

Fear. Fear is a more intense emotion and usually arises when you have concerns that something bad will happen as a result of your young adult's actions or inactions. Fear is an alert mechanism, but we have to be careful not to overreact. Suppose your child is promiscuous, being abused by her boyfriend, or doing drugs. You know that this is highly unhealthy and risky behavior that may result in physical harm, prison, or worse. It's painful for parents to watch the one they love make horrible decisions and suffer. Fear may prompt you to intervene through tough love, paying for counseling, or protecting younger children from the danger of the adult child's presence.

Another kind of fear is more slippery: the fear that your young adult may be at risk of losing his immortal soul. As serious as this is, there usually is little that a parent can do to save the soul of another person. Christians believe that Jesus has already done this.

Your young adult may not go to church or believe in God. Will these things actually cause the loving God we believe in to abandon our child? We may not understand how God works, but if *we* believe, we must trust that God loves our child even more than we do and will take care of things in ways and at times that we cannot know or control.

Fear might have to be tempered by patience as you wait around (sometimes for a very long time) for your young adult to return to her senses. Remember the father in the parable of the prodigal son and hold fast to your unconditional love for your child, but be ready to pick up the pieces when she returns.

Anger. Anger is the most intense and potentially the most dangerous emotion that parents might feel. At its extreme, anger can result in physical or verbal abuse. Physical abuse is unacceptable, and screaming and belittling can hurt just as deeply as physical abuse. Perhaps you're furious with him for squandering the money you lent him to pay off his credit card. Perhaps you're angry because he announced that he's an atheist and you want to make a sarcastic remark about taking him out of your will. As the degree of anger increases, so should your consideration of counseling or anger management classes.

As an emotion, anger comes unbidden. Although sometimes the anger is understandable because a grievous wrong has been done, acting on it in a way that hurts others is unacceptable. Get the help you need. Often, the worst harm that anger causes is not to another, but to yourself. Nursing anger can cause you to be unhappy; you become a mean, cranky person to be around. You'll lose friends, family, and respect for yourself. Following are some strategies to help you move beyond your anger, whether with your young adult, with God, or with yourself.

Force yourself to see the good. I once was having difficulty seeing anything but problems with one of my kids. A spiritual advisor asked me to do an exercise in which I had to identify one or more positive characteristic about this child that wouldn't be followed by a "but." Since I very much loved this child, I thought this would be simple–until I tried it. The "buts" were harder to shed than I had imagined.

For example, some "positives" that would not pass muster are: "My son is very creative, but I wish he would direct that creativity to something other than video games." Or, "My daughter is very beautiful, but that has gotten her into trouble with boyfriends." Or, "My son is very artistic, but that temperament makes it hard for him to get and hold a job that will support him. Besides, I worry about some of the friends he has surrounded himself with who don't have a work ethic." Force yourself to come up with a positive trait that doesn't have any negative conditions on it. For example, "My daughter is selfless in the way she spends herself on causes that contribute to the common good." You don't ever have to repeat your compliment to your son or daughter, although you might decide to do so. The point is to start training your mind to think more positively. The emotions may follow.

Pray more. If your anger is primarily with God, it is OK to yell and wail at God. That is what many of the psalms are about–people pouring their hearts out to God, often in unfiltered anger. God can take it. Leave it to God to eventually defuse that anger and draw you close. Is there a psalm that expresses your feelings at this time?

Forgive yourself. If your anger is primarily at yourself for having made a mistake, remember that God does not require perfection but rather a heart that is soft enough to hurt and a willingness to be faithful to your child and to God. Although feeling anger is not a sin itself, Catholics can find healing in the sacrament of reconciliation as God works through the priest to reassure us of God's love. If it's been a while since you went to confession, your anger may be a prompt to return.

Get professional help if necessary. Sometimes anger just keeps eating away at us, and it's hard to let go of it because, in a sense, we like being angry. Of course, we would never admit this, but anger serves the purpose of keeping the wrongs of others in front of us. We can obsess about a hurt or an offense rather than moving on to solutions or taking care of more important business. It's easier to nurse anger than to do the work of moving on.

6. THE VIRTUE OF LISTENING

Then he called the crowd to him and said to them, "Listen and understand." (Matthew 15:10)

Now the Lord came and stood there, calling as before, "Samuel! Samuel!" And Samuel said, "Speak, for your servant is listening." (1 Samuel 3:10)

Although most of us think we are good listeners, the truth is that most of us aren't. (I have this on the good authority of my husband.) Sometimes people think that just because they don't talk much, they must be good listeners. Following is a summary of classic listening rules that might help you deepen your growth in this virtue.

Listening is not the same as being quiet. Yes, listening starts with being quiet, but when sensitive or contentious issues are on the table, it helps to go to that old standby—active listening. You know the drill: After listening to your young adult for a little bit, you try to digest what they are saying and feeling and summarize it. "So, you felt embarrassed when I brought up your lack of church attendance in front of the relatives?" Or "So, you feel discounted when I act like I know what's best for you?"

Don't listen with your answer running. Sometimes when we feel strongly about something and find ourselves in an argument, it is tempting to only half listen to the other person while we conjure rebuttals to bolster our case. This is a handy skill if you are on a debate team. Your child, however, is not an opponent. Don't make your relationship one long debate. (Don't ask me how I know this.) Honor the person you are listening to with your full attention. Pause, think, then respond.

Avoid SSS (Self-Summarizing Syndrome). This is one I learned from my husband. Since we both like to win arguments, as soon as he takes a breath, I'm tempted to respond with a more detailed (or perhaps just repetitive) version of the argument I made a moment ago. This does not add new information, it just adds fuel to the fire. This tactic is a close cousin of nagging, and you should especially avoid it with your young adult.

Listen to wise friends who are a stage ahead of you in parenting. Listening and sharing with close friends (or a professional counselor, if appropriate) can help you sort out what is worth getting upset about and what isn't. If your spouse or a really close friend is willing to let you vent and not try to fix the problem, you may find that can defuse negative emotions. Just don't overdo it.

Listen to God. Meeting God in church is an opportunity for God to enter our lives directly, but it does not necessarily mean we are listening. Through prayer, we can not only pour out our hearts to God and ask for things we need, but we can know God's presence, comfort, and will if we are quiet and attentive. God's message may not come directly at the time of prayer. It may come later, through the words of a trusted friend, a fortuitous experience, or an insight that pops into our head. Often it's only later that we connect the dots and recognize that a prayer has been answered or reframed in a way we had not expected. If we keep open our communication with God, we will recognize that sacred presence when we need it.

7. THE VIRTUE OF GIVING COUNSEL

And if I give you advice, you will not listen to me. (Jeremiah 38:15)

When parenting young adults, wisdom primarily takes the form of discerning when we should intervene and when we shouldn't. Your young adult's life may be going smoothly and so you feel no urge to intervene. Plus, the icing on the cake is that he's actively involved in a faith community. But many young adults do not fit this ideal. At this point in your parenting life, you should have made the final transition from being responsible for your child to being a collaborator in his search for the meaning of life. Actions and emotions, however, often lag behind the will in making this shift.

Becoming a mentor or collaborator with your young adult is akin to going from being a parent to being a godparent. Parents have the day-to-day direct responsibility for raising their children. Godparents, on the other hand, aren't the disciplinarians or teachers of prayers and transporters to church; they're simply nearby, spiritually, if not physically. A godparent is often in a position to be an outside influence without being a nag. Thus, your job at this point may be to shift from biological parenthood to baptismal godparenthood.

So how you move from parent to godparent without being either too disengaged or too enmeshed? The disengaged parent says, "It's your life. I don't care." The enmeshed parent says, "This is what I believe you should do." The godparent, or mentor parent, might say, "This is what I believe, but it is up to you. I will love and respect you whatever you do." Just as collaborators in business are peers but with different areas of expertise, the collaborating parent must cultivate the art of being supportive while no longer being the one in charge.

When unsure of whether you're interfering or just trying to be helpful, ask yourself this fundamental question: Would my action promote my young adult's dependence or independence? For example, will signing up the newly married couple for my *Marriage Moment* e-mails convey confidence in the couple's ability to lead their own life? Probably not. Let them subscribe themselves. Be careful not to be over responsible, no matter how well-meaning the gesture. On the other hand, if your daughter has expressed the desire to seek marriage counseling, would it be too controlling to provide a list of reputable counselors? It depends. If this becomes a project for you, let go and just give her the name of a reputable counseling agency. Providing names of several recommended counselors, however, could be the jump start she needs to make the initial appointment. (Don't you dare make that appointment!)

In money matters, assisting with tuition payments can build your son's capacity to earn a higher income in the future, while paying off his credit card debt may perpetuate his living above his means in the future.

In matters of faith, it may be disconcerting if he walks to the beat of his own drummer—and that happens to be on Sunday morning, in a park, with nothing that looks like traditional religion. What's a parent to do? Give up and resign yourself to being a mediocre parent in the faith department? Cajole, bribe, or guilt him into becoming a regular church-goer? E-mail religious essays or sign him up for the diocesan newspaper? Join him in dropping out? Resort to prayer as a last resort?

You have so much experience and hard-won wisdom to share—on jobs, marriage, and life in general—that it's hard to sit back and watch your young adult make a decision that you think is unwise or might backfire. Yet that discipline is part of what you presumably learned when working on our first virtue, the silence of words. There are times, however, when giving counsel is requested, appropriate, and helpful. How do you do this most effectively?

Advise only when asked, except. . . . It is a no-brainer that people are most receptive to advice if they request it themselves. The reverse is also true: People usually resent unsolicited advice, as well as the person giving it. Given these truisms, is it ever appropriate and helpful to give unasked-for advice to your young adult? I deal with what to do if you aren't thrilled with your young adult's choice of mate in chapter three, but what about after they are married? Unless your son is on a seriously self-destructive path, it's best not to offer unsolicited advice. One exception to the "wait until you're asked" rule is when there is life-threatening danger to your young adult, his spouse, or their children. If, therefore, you notice or suspect abuse, it's your responsibility to say something. Otherwise, if it's simply a case of something you dislike or find annoying, hold your tongue.

How to give counsel when asked. First, you pray–not only for your young adult, but that God may speak words of wisdom through you and that you may convey your unconditional love. Presumably, you would then use the standard communication tools of "I statements" and sharing feelings. For example, "I feel sad that going to church is not important to you. I feel a bit rejected since I highly value faith in God. I doubt that you mean it that way. Help me understand what you really do believe about God, faith, and spirituality." Hopefully, you've already incorporated these skills into your daily communication.

8. The Virtue of Renewal of Resolutions

> So let us not grow weary in doing what is right, for we will
> reap at harvest-time, if we do not give up. (Galatians 6:9)

You hope that when your young adult marries, he will be happy and the marriage will last forever. Although you can't guarantee this, you can model an honest growing marriage yourself. This is an opportunity to check the health of your own marriage and renew your commitment to your own spouse.

Renewing your commitment to your own marriage. If you have adult children, you probably have been married for quite a while yourself. Even if you are in a second marriage, time and age bring the temptation to take each other for granted or to get into ruts. One of the best indirect actions you can take to strengthen your young adult's marriage is to pay attention to your own. This may mean taking a second honeymoon or simply renewing your commitment to speak kindly and gently to your spouse. To reinforce your resolve and refresh your marriage, consider taking advantage of marriage enrichment opportunities. These include activities such as reading books about marriage, getting my weekly Marriage Moment e-mails (see Bibliography), or attending an evening talk, day-long program, or weekend marriage enrichment retreat. Marriage Encounter is one of the most widely known weekend marriage enrichment programs. (See www.ForYourMarriage.org for listings of the most common national programs.) Churches often sponsor marriage enrichment events of a local nature. Don't be afraid to give it a try. It not only will renew your own marriage, it models good preventive practices for your young adult.

Being faithful when divorced, widowed, or in a troubled marriage. Regrettably, not every marriage is happy and lasting. What do you do when, despite your original commitment, your own marriage has not worked out as you hoped?

• If you're still married–but not happily–you can still take several steps to model healthy relationship skills. Retrouvaille and The Third Option are both programs for couples in troubled marriages (see Bibliography). These programs are not a substitute for counseling, but often they can reinforce counseling or motivate couples to make needed changes in their relationship. Another route is to seek marriage counseling. If you've tried counseling and didn't like it, try again with a different counselor. Finding a good counselor is often a matter of finding the right match. Remember, your young adults are watching, and knowing that you're getting help for your marriage makes it more likely they'll consider this mature approach to problem solving if they need it.

- If you're divorced, renewal of vows may take the form of renewing your commitment not to speak ill of your ex-spouse. It also can be a commitment to honest and responsible sexual integrity, if you choose to date. Being faithful to your responsibilities to your other children or grandchildren who need your care are other dimensions of renewal of resolutions. The commitment may not always be to a spouse, but any time you model being a person of your word, it conveys a message of mature commitment to the young married couple.
- If you're single or widowed, renew your resolution to be a person of integrity and your word.

9. THE VIRTUE OF PEACEMAKING

Blessed are the peacemakers, for they will be called children of God. (Matthew 5:9)

As a married person (or person in any type of familial relationship), you already know that one of the virtues of marriage is peacemaking. It doesn't mean that couples, siblings, and parents and children don't fight about their disagreements, but rather this virtue is about taking inevitable disagreements and learning how to work through them to a point where both parties feel that they've achieved a fair and satisfactory resolution. Perhaps you have a healthy, satisfying marriage, and you have long ago settled the bones of contention between you and your spouse. On the other hand, maybe you're divorced or still struggling to make peace with that person you love who shares your bed. Either way, the skills and attitudes of peacemaking fundamental to successful marriage need to be transferred to your relationship with your young adult. Following are some places to start.

Banish discouraging or pessimistic attitudes. Sure, you love your young adult. Most of us, however, are all too aware of the weaknesses of our offspring, just as we know the flaws of our spouses, if we're married. After all, you've been around each other long enough to observe more than enough mistakes, bad decisions, and animosity. When there is an issue about which you and your son disagree, it's time to let go of the memories of past offenses, past faults, and past negative emotions, and turn toward what is loveable about him. This is so you can summon your underlying love and assume honest and honorable motives. It doesn't mean you have unrealistic expectations, but it does mean that you give him the benefit of the doubt and do not deem him a failure because you disagree about how he set up his household or negotiates conflicts with his girlfriend.

Listen again with clean ears. Once the filter of past negative attitudes has been lifted, it's time to listen again to the positions, arguments, or desires of your young adult. It might be helpful to review the virtue of listening, especially the part about "listening with your answer running."

Walk in the other's shoes. As a peacemaker, you don't have to *agree* with the other's position or belief, but trying to *understand* the circumstances of your young adult is the first step to getting along. What pressures, fears, or anxieties is she dealing with? Once you honestly understand the situation, the next step is to communicate that understanding. Too often we believe we understand, but this understanding is not effectively conveyed to our young adult. While the active listening technique—"So you feel that living with your boyfriend before marriage will help you confirm your compatibility and safeguard against divorce"—may seem silly, it works amazingly well if it is sincere. Your daughter needs to know that you understand her position before her ears can open to hearing *yours*. Ask nonjudgmental questions about the values she holds, and honestly consider what piece of truth might be contained therein.

Compromise. Once both parent and young adult genuinely believe that they are understood, there is room for negotiation and compromise. Of course, you would not compromise your integrity or heartfelt values, but remember that we are responsible for the *process* we used in raising our children, *not the outcome*. (See the Conclusion for more on this.) We cannot control what our young adults think, believe, or do. We can punish them when they're children, but once they're adults, our punishment, our whining about how they fail to respect us, and our threats to disown them can only bring temporary or superficial change while destroying the parent-adult child relationship. On our deathbeds, it is the relationship that we will cherish and the unconditional love we gave upon which we will be judged.

Having set aside the fear of being untrue to yourself if you compromise, how do you compromise authentically? It's not just a matter of finding the middle ground as in labor negotiations, but rather, finding how we both can get some of our needs met while not violating our consciences. If your son is living with his girlfriend, you can control where they sleep when visiting you, but you must refrain from bombarding them with preachy literature and words. If you want him to marry in a church but he's not actively practicing a faith, you can support the love that brings him and his fiancée together and pray that someday faith may reawaken in them, at which time they could have their marriage blessed in a church.

When the disagreement is not between you and your child but between you and your spouse. The rule here is the same as when your young adult was a child: Work it out between you and your spouse first. If it's not important, decide to exercise self-restraint, and hold your tongue. If it is a disagreement that absolutely *must* be voiced, you and your spouse can jointly and calmly express your views, acknowledging that you disagree and that you will honor whatever decision your young adult makes.

When the disagreement is between your child and her spouse, or between your child and siblings. Better to stay out of these squabbles. It is not your business. When you become a third party to others' disputes, the result is never good. If necessary, suggest a professional counselor as a neutral third party.

When in doubt, go back to prayer. As a loving parent, continue to pray for your young adult. As our young adults mature, our prayer must also mature. Instead of praying that the young adults practice our faith, pray that they will recognize God's presence in their lives. Trust that God will know the time and way to speak to their hearts better than you can ever dictate. But most important, pray for the grace of parenthood. This means that we ask God to calm our fears and to help us in being a guide.

10. THE VIRTUE OF JOY

> And Mary said, "My soul magnifies the Lord, and my spirit rejoices in God my Savior, for he has looked with favor on the lowliness of his servant. Surely, from now on all generations will call me blessed; for the Mighty One has done great things for me, and holy is his name." (Luke 1:46–49)

Not all parents become grandparents, but many do and joy usually comes unbidden to new grandparents. It may not seem necessary to cultivate it as a virtue because it is so automatic. But you know from raising your own children that parenting is also fraught with worry and fears for the health and well-being of such a fragile new human being. Joy reminds us to look past our fears and worries to remember the awesome gift of this new life.

Use joy to counter fears. Every time a worry creeps into your consciousness, decide whether it is anything you can actually do anything about – other than worry. If action is not possible or practical, train yourself to replace the fear with joy, or at least acceptance of the current situation. Focus on the wonder and goodness of this grandchild. As usual, pray. If prayer is still clouded by fear, pray your fears and ask God to fill your heart with hope to be able to see the good. Joy is the virtue that balances your worries and helps you to continue loving under less than perfect conditions – which is all the time.

11. The Virtue of Balancing Service and Energy

"You are the salt of the earth;.... You are the light of the world...let your light shine before others, so that they may see your good works and give glory to your Father in heaven." (Matthew 5:13, 14, 16)

And after he had dismissed the crowds, he went up the mountain by himself to pray. (Matthew 14:23)

Service to others should be a component of the spiritual life at any age, but by the time you have an adult child and perhaps even grandchildren, usually your own parenting demands are lessening. Just as children embark upon stages of life that require incredible physical energy, you may generally find your physical energy levels waning. Working wiser can compensate for this. The secret of how to accomplish this is a matter of balance. Just as Jesus periodically took time away from the crowds to pray during his public ministry years, we have to find ways to be both reflective and active.

Franciscan author Fr. Richard Rohr describes this as being committed to both action and contemplation. You can ask the chicken and egg question about which comes first—the action or the contemplation—but the answer is always the same: Both are usually present in an authentic spiritual life. We may alternate from one emphasis to the other depending on the day, month, or year, but action without contemplation usually ends up as simply busyness or spinning our wheels. Contemplation without action leads to hollow platitudes and pious self-righteousness.

In terms of action, some grandparents take on an active role in the daily raising of their grandchildren through necessity or desire. If this is not your situation, you have the challenge of how to use your discretionary time in service both to your expanding family and the community at large. Let's look at family commitments first.

Service to your family. Most grandparents are happy to babysit. The issue is how much and under what conditions. It may be difficult to determine the boundaries of your time and energy. Here is where you need to honestly assess your capabilities and how much free service you can responsibly give. Some grandparents are the backup babysitters for when a child is sick and the regular day-care provider will not accept the child. Others generously offer to be the regular, daily childcare provider. Some grandparents live at a distance and can do neither, but they welcome visits and support the parents by being a place of respite. Several creative and talented grandparents I know have set up what they call "Granny's camp." This is a week in which a grandparent offers to take one or more grandchildren and devotes the time to camp-like activities–arts and crafts, games, field trips, and so on. It becomes a bonding time for the grandparent and grandchild and a welcome break for the parent.

Know your limitations, however, and determine your boundaries, because a grandparent who provides childcare out of guilt is not a happy, joy-filled grandparent. This may keep your child unduly dependent on you, and you may develop feelings of resentment. This is not good for you, your adult child, or your grandchild.

Service to the community. A wonderful side effect of becoming an empty-nester is that there are many worthy works and volunteer efforts for which you have more time. It may be that you are still heavily involved in the work world; in fact, you may be reaching the peak years of your career. If you are semi- or fully retired, you may finally have time to plunge into significant volunteer work. This is the blessing and the challenge of being freed from the demands of daily parenting. It is a blessing because the community needs your wisdom, experience, and time. It is a challenge because it is easy to become overcommitted. Boards, committees, and projects covet your presence.

Grandparents sometimes have more discretionary money than discretionary time. For example, Mike and Mary Andrews annually give each of their young adults a Christmas check to be donated to a charity of their choice in the name of their grandchild. As the grandchildren get older, the check will be given directly to them to make the decision. Time is always a precious gift, but teaching generosity can be done in many ways.

You certainly could fill your discretionary time with personal recreation and socializing. Such pursuits are not bad, and in many ways you deserve time to do whatever you want. After all, you put in a lot of years parenting and working. But, if personal pleasure is all you devote yourself to during your newly found time, you may be selling yourself short and filling your days primarily with small talk. Yes, lavish attention on your grandchildren, but consider saving some time for children who do not have grandparents to smother them with love.

12. THE VIRTUE OF SELF-SACRIFICE

> Very truly, I tell you, when you were younger, you used to fasten your own belt and to go wherever you wished. But when you grow old, you will stretch out your hands, and someone else will fasten a belt around you and take you where you do not wish to go. (John 21:18)

> He also told this parable to some who trusted in themselves that they were righteous and regarded others with contempt: "Two men went up to the temple to pray, one a Pharisee and the other a tax collector. The Pharisee, standing by himself, was praying thus, 'God, I thank you that I am not like other people: thieves, rogues, adulterers, or even like this tax collector. I fast twice a week; I give a tenth of all

my income.' But the tax collector, standing far off, would not even look up to heaven, but was beating his breast and saying, 'God, be merciful to me, a sinner!' I tell you, this man went down to his home justified rather than the other; for all who exalt themselves will be humbled, but all who humble themselves will be exalted." (Luke 18:9-14)

To a great extent, maturing in life and faith is a journey from selfishness to self-sacrifice. Of necessity, children focus on physical development and coming into their own identity. As they age, they begin to understand that others have needs, too, and life is not "just about me." Marriage expands this awareness to another beloved person, and parenthood helps us to understand how a person would give one's life for another.

Grandparenthood is a continuation of this journey. We can get consumed with our care for others. Of course, there are also times of dependence, when we recognize our diminishing physical abilities and ineptitude at text messaging, video games, or the latest technological gadget. Both our increased selflessness and reliance on others are manifestations of letting go of our need for power. We continue to grow in awareness that life is not "all about me." Ironically, it is this movement toward greater self-sacrifice that increases our ability to influence and brings us closer to Jesus' ultimate self-sacrifice on the cross. Witnessing self-sacrifice can prompt the seed of faith in others –if done without drawing attention to ourselves.

Focus on your core beliefs. As we get older and want to focus our attention on others more than ourselves, the specific practices of religion often give way to a deeper understanding of the faith that was the source of religion in the first place–at least that's the way it works for believers searching for a closer relationship with God.

In the middle of our faith journey, it's easy to be distracted by questions–whose religion is best, whether or not there is a limbo, the rubrics and language of religious services–that we lose sight of what is really important. The peripherals may make for some entertaining conversation, but these topics will pass. To be mentors to our young adults in faith, we must first *ourselves* recognize the basic meaning of the paschal mystery of death and resurrection. As we face the many mini-deaths of life–the death of a spouse, the death of a relationship, or simply a hurt inflicted by a friend–the spiritual message that forgiveness and resurrection are possible starts to sink in. The paschal mystery of life, death, and rebirth gives us hope to go on and love through it. If you don't know the core beliefs of your religion, it's time for some adult faith formation through classes or reading. Encourage your young adults to do the same so that their religious education does not stagnate at a high school level when they arc adults in othcr faccts of their lives.

Strip yourself of biases and self-righteousness. Part of changing your focus from the self to the other means letting go of being right–even if you *are* right. To draw others to God, we must enter the other's world and understand it from the inside. This means recognizing any biases we may have and letting go of them so that we can understand the needs and pains of others–those we love and those we love to hate. For example, you may have been raised to think that it is immoral to be an atheist, a homosexual, a Democrat, a Republican, whatever. Biases often melt away when we get to know the other person as a unique individual.

To relate to your young adult's world, you might need to lose some of your preconceptions about other people and right and wrong. This doesn't mean that you give up your morals or beliefs, but rather that you stretch yourself to see what part of the truth another person may hold. Even if you remain firmly convinced of the rightness of your positions and beliefs–and, presumably, most of them have been founded on rock and should not be abandoned– letting go of self-righteousness allows you to love the other unconditionally, as God does.

Be humble. If you've been successful at stripping yourself of self-righteousness, you may, de facto, already be humble, since this virtue often comes indirectly. It might even be oxymoronic to actually strive to be humble. Rather, humility generally comes from recognizing one's honest relationship to God. We are not the Creator, the Savior, or the Sustainer of Life. Indeed, we can let go of those responsibilities, since God has already taken care of them. Remember, however, that it is false humility to belittle ourselves or not use our talents, since God "does not make junk." When we have the self-awareness to know that we're not the center of the universe but that we have a responsibility to use the gifts and talents given us to honor and support God's work on earth, we will, as the Shaker song goes, "come 'round right."

13. The Virtue of Wisdom

> But O that God would speak,
> and open his lips to you,
> and that he would tell you the secrets of wisdom!
> For wisdom is many-sided.
> Know then that God exacts of
> you less than your guilt deserves. (Job 11:5–6)

> Listen to advice and accept instruction,
> that you may gain wisdom for the future. (Proverbs 19:20)

One of the signs of wisdom is recognizing when to listen to your intuition and when to get outside help. Wisdom needs both an inside and outside game. Wisdom comes from within (your own experience) and from without (listening to the experiences of others.) Make enough quiet in your life to notice the wisdom of your heart and your lived experience. Another name for this quiet is prayer.

Add to this the wisdom of others. If your daughter has a homosexual orientation, has grown up with a disability, or has an addiction or a mental illness, I presume you've already read background material to help you understand her situation and needs. If she's a single parent, divorced, or simply taking some time finding her next step in life, the resources you need may be less factual and more personal, such as the support of other parents who have walked in your shoes. There's a place for both learning from experts and the informal support of friends. The double-teaming approach of using both resources usually works best.

Be wise enough to know when to seek professional help. There are times, however, when even the best friend, book, DVD, or website isn't enough. Consulting with a professional counselor with expertise in the issue you face is a sign of wisdom, not weakness. It takes humility to seek counsel, but it is the smart thing to do. The first step is to find the right counselor for your need and personality. All too often I hear people say, "I tried counseling and it didn't work." Of course, for various reasons, counseling occasionally may be ineffective; but most often it is simply that the counselor-client match isn't a good one. The counselor may have the proper credentials, but the client just doesn't feel understood or feel that he's making any progress. Of course, the other barrier might be that the client is not receptive to hearing another side to the story.

When seeking counsel, remember that, even though what prompted you to seek the advice of another may have been a difficult situation with your young adult, still, you're not in a counseling session to change her. Counseling can help you understand her better, but any change or action you take is for *you*. Blowing off steam to God is also acceptable, although you might also try to listen to God's counsel through Scripture.

14. The Virtue of Unconditional Love

Be merciful, just as your Father is merciful. Do not judge, and you will not be judged; do not condemn, and you will not be condemned. Forgive, and you will be forgiven; give, and it will be given to you. (Luke 6:36–37)

> As God's chosen ones, holy and beloved, clothe yourselves with compassion, kindness, humility, meekness, and patience. Bear with one another and, if anyone has a complaint against another, forgive each other; just as the Lord has forgiven you, so you also must forgive. (Colossians 3:12–13)

An old story goes, "A man tried everything he could think of to eradicate the weeds in his lawn. Finally, in desperation, he wrote to the Department of Agriculture, asking advice and listing every method he had tried. He received a reply that said, 'We suggest you learn to love them!'"

I have no idea whether this story actually happened. As spiritual storyteller Megan McKenna says, "Everything in the Bible is true. Some of it actually happened." The point of the weeds story, however, still carries truth. Ultimately, we keep striving to love our sons and daughters unconditionally, despite their flaws, mistakes, or outright rejection. Sometimes it helps to cry. Then we pick ourselves up and start all over again to love. Christians have the sacrifice of Jesus on the cross to attest to the cost of unconditional love. God never said it would be easy. God just promised to be with us.

Compassion. One route to unconditional love is to nurture compassion. This takes mentally putting yourself into the shoes of your young adult. (See the virtue of peacemaking for a refresher on this.) You may not agree with your son's decision or lifestyle, but the more you understand it, the more you can feel his pain or what drove him to make certain choices. For example, Bill Hirt, a committed pacifist, struggled to understand his son, Tim, who was enamored with wrestling and liked to watch World Wrestling Federation programs. Despite Bill's dislike for this sport, he decided to join Tim in his passion. He even took Tim and a friend to see an out-of-town wrestling match. Bill opened his mind to what interested his son in order to build the parent-child relationship.

If your young adult is homosexual, remind yourself that this is *not* a choice. People don't voluntarily subject themselves to prejudice. The more you can appreciate the emotional turmoil she may be experiencing, the more you can support and help her find acceptance and peace of mind and heart. If you're perceived as judgmental or out of touch, it becomes hard for you to be part of a healing partnership with her.

Loyalty. Family is sometimes defined as the place you go when there's no place else to go. Family loyalty is good. But loyalty doesn't mean rescuing young adults from the consequences of their actions. This keeps them dependent and always looking for the next bailout. Loyalty can also mean doing what's in their best *long-range interests*, even though they may not like you or your decision in the short run. You are being loyal to your child's future. This brings us to tough love.

Tough love. Tough love is tough–both for the giver and the receiver. It means that sometimes parents will have to tell their young adults that they can no longer live at home–not because they aren't loved but because they need to learn to live on their own. Or it may be a decision based on a parent's assessment of the needs of other family members. Perhaps the young adult puts other family members in danger by continued illegal or immoral behavior. Such difficult decisions are best made after consulting family members, a counselor, and experts. Remember that you're only putting an end to enabling the behavior. Your *love* doesn't end.

15. THE VIRTUE OF FORGIVENESS

> Then Jesus said, "Father, forgive them; for they do not know what they are doing." (Luke 23:34)

Sooner or later, everyone has reason to forgive. It may be a small infraction such as an insult or someone cutting you off in traffic. To need to forgive is part of being human. To be willing to do it is much more challenging. First, forgiving someone does not erase the wrong that might have been done. It doesn't mean that you now agree with the other person's position or action. It also doesn't mean that you can automatically forget the offense.

Forgiveness is strongly related to the virtue of patience. Healing from being wronged can take a long time, sometimes forever. Be patient with the offender–even if it's you–since long-established habits die slowly.

Forgiveness of others. Perhaps your young adult has indeed done something terribly wrong–at least in your eyes and maybe also in society's eyes. Listen to the counsel of a mother from Michigan whose son is in prison for a heinous murder: "It's been terrible for all of us. I am inspired by saint stories. St. Moses the Black often comes to mind when I think about my son's imprisonment. It's a hard thing to think of a child facing life imprisonment, which is why I cling to St. Moses, who actually came out of prison. But I'm also realistic. I know that love covers a multitude of sins." We who live in this difficult situation must love and persevere, remembering what Jesus said: "[God] has anointed me to bring good news to the poor. He has sent me to proclaim release to the captives and recovery of sight to the blind, to let the oppressed go free" (Luke 4: 18).

One of the beauties of the Catholic tradition is that there is a saint for just about any circumstance. For example, parents who are facing their young adult's unexpected pregnancy might turn to Sts. Anne and Joachim, the parents of Mary, the Mother of God. Surely they would understand the confusion and anguish of hearing the disturbing news that your unwed child is expecting.

Forgiving others is a teaching of most world religions and reinforced by the Golden Rule and the Our Father; even modern psychology weighs in on the efficacy of forgiveness. Numerous scientific studies indicate that forgiveness is healthy; it results in less depression, lower blood pressure and heart rates and many other health benefits. Thus, we have another example of how grace builds on nature.

No matter how strong your disappointment in your young adult or how grievous her behavior, remember that as a parent you're responsible for the process you used in raising your children, not the outcome. They have free will and must be free to make their own mistakes. Even if in hindsight you recognize that you would have, could have, should have done something differently, I have found it to be almost universally true that most parents did the best they could, with the knowledge they had at the time, and under the circumstances that they faced. *Now* you may know better, but leave judgment to God, who sees the whole picture and has the ability to heal.

Forgiveness of self. Forgiveness is often a long process and frequently leads parents back to the self. You may ask yourself, "Could I have done more to save my son from the problems he's facing?" The Michigan parents above with a son in prison not only had to forgive their son but also deal with forgiving themselves: "It doesn't serve anyone to hide under a cloak of shame and guilt. My husband and I are not sinless, nor do we pretend to be. We see how choices we made affected our children, for better or worse. We have to be brave enough to face our failures. And braver still to do what Christ would have us do, whether or not we get the response wanted from our children. Sometimes, we have to let go and trust God for all of it."

It's easy to say "trust God"; it's harder to live this attitude daily when we continue to see the ramifications of bad decisions or unhealthy lifestyles. If forgiveness doesn't come easily, support groups can put you in touch with other parents who face similar challenges, and professional counseling can be helpful. As always, turn back to God in prayer, relinquishing your worries, inadequacies, and feelings of self-blame to God's loving mercy.

When *you* are the one who needs help. Sometimes the tables are turned and the roles of parent and child reverse. This can be a blessing, as described in chapter two, when your children generously share their talents with you. There may be other times, however, when you need help from your child and feel uncomfortable asking, or you do ask and your child resists or resents it. How much do you push then? Do you just suffer in silence? For example, perhaps your young adult is in better financial shape than you are, but you're too proud to ask for a loan. Or you may simply want some help with the yard work or moving some furniture.

Ideally, extended families have a natural reciprocity in which, as the children grow up, they notice when a parent needs help or at least readily give help when requested. When this doesn't happen naturally, you can either beat yourself up for being a bad parent and not teaching your children generosity, or you can give yourself a good talking to. For example, tell yourself something like, "Well, maybe I did teach them generosity and it just didn't take, or maybe I was too indulgent. If so, that's water over the dam now and I can't change it. What I *can* change is my attitude. I can swallow my pride and ask for help–without laying a guilt trip on my child. If I still get no response, I will ask a friend to help or hire the job out and let it go."

PRAYER

Prayer may not be a virtue in the strict sense, but it is certainly the glue that keeps many parents from falling apart. Having children can drive one to exhaustion; having young adults can drive one more deeply into prayer. Many parents pray for their children every day. Prayer is an outlet when nothing else seems to work. When we're at our wit's end, we pray. To whom besides God could we go?

Some may view prayer, however, as a crutch–as the way that weak humans deal with the uncertainties of life. Yes, perhaps prayer is a crutch. The eyes of faith, however, lead me to regard prayer as a crutch that a wise God gives believers so we may find comfort, clarity, and sanity.

Prayer isn't magic. There is something very healing about taking a fear or worry to a higher power. The process of forming a prayer, in our mind or aloud, helps us to clarify our thoughts and feelings. This is part of the process of discernment. The quiet of consciously sitting, kneeling, or standing in God's presence gives us the space to listen and recognize our dependence on God.

"Thinkin' and Prayin'." Remember the song made popular by Dusty Springfield in the 1960s that begins: "Wishin', and hopin', and thinkin', and prayin'"? The song explores how teenage girls try to get boys to notice them. Thankfully, you're past those days, but parents of young adults sometimes fixate on the "wishin' and hopin'" stage when they need to move on to the "thinkin' and prayin'" stage.

Prayer can be divided into two broad categories: private prayer and community prayer. Although one could offer a Mass or a petition at Mass for young adults, most of the praying that we parents do for our children is probably private. Some people prefer spontaneous prayers to be straight from the heart; others prefer memorized or repetitive prayers, such as the rosary. Still others prefer just to sit in God's presence either at home, in nature, or in a quiet church. Some use Scripture or spiritual reading as a prayer prompt; others sit and meditate. Prayers can be spoken or nonverbal communication with God. The only thing necessary for prayer is that it comes from our hearts.

The beauty of prayer is that you can't do it incorrectly. If you intend to talk to God, God will lead you. One thing I've learned through my own prayer is that I might start with a very specific request of God—for example, "Dear God, help my son get this job he has applied for," or "Help my daughter find a loving spouse." That kind of prayer is fine; it's direct, and I'm sure God knows what I mean. An interesting thing often happens, however, when I keep bringing that same concern to God's attention. I might start thinking that the job I want my daughter to get might not really be the right fit or that marriage might not be my son's calling. As I keep praying, my prayer becomes broader and usually ends up as, "Dear God, I put my child in your hands. You know what is best. Help me to love him as unconditionally as you do."

We are not the masters of our universe. Putting life in perspective like this helps us to see that we are not God. We are not responsible for saving the world or our children. We are humble vehicles of God's grace, but salvation does not depend on us. Remembering this relieves us of a heavy burden.

We might not be totally confident that God exists and listens to our prayer. Still, the act of praying is an act of belief and has a calming function, even when done in doubt or imperfectly. It may not be a silver bullet, but prayer was the one thing that parents I surveyed overwhelmingly found solace in during difficult times with their young adults. Sometimes the prayer was in the form of going to Mass more often, saying novenas or rosaries, or other such traditional devotions. Other times it was repeated heartfelt entreaties to God whenever they thought of their son or daughter. Sometimes it was through reflecting on Scripture, carving out a time of private contemplative prayer every day, or even listening to the counsel of other wise parents. Never underestimate the power of prayer–for clearing the head, for healing, for listening, for grace.

Praying and waiting (or, everybody loves St. Monica). St. Monica kept popping up in many of my survey returns. If she is already a faithful "go-to" person for you, you need no introduction. For those unfamiliar with her story, St. Monica of Hippo, born in North Africa in AD 333, was the mother of St. Augustine. Although she was a Christian, she married Patritius, an adulterer with no religion and a violent temper. Their son, Augustine, was no pearl either.

He was wayward, lived with a mistress, and, as he himself admits in his writings, was lazy. Despite these transgressions, eventually, through St. Monica's prayer, patience, and perseverance, both Patritius and Augustine became Christians. If you want to pray to God through a person who has "been there, done that," St. Monica is your woman.

But maybe it's been a while since you had a heart-to-heart with God. How do you start to pray? Certainly, there are many ways to pray, as summarized under the virtue of listening, above. For those of you who feel awkward or rusty at prayer, let me suggest some places to start.

Waiting for Godot. If you have ever seen or read Samuel Beckett's play, "Waiting for Godot," you may be able to identify with the two characters who are waiting for the mysterious and unknown Godot. Some suggest that Godot is an allusion to God, but regardless, waiting to feel God's presence or experience an answer to prayer can be a very long wait. Not only do we wait on God, but we find ourselves at times waiting for a young adult to make a change we think is important. We may be right; we may not.

There's another kind of waiting, however, and that's the self-discipline of waiting on yourself. Just because I know something or want to give some good advice to my child doesn't mean I should say it now. For example, during our daughter's college years, I would periodically check in with her about the "church thing." Was she going? Didn't she want to offer her flute playing to the local parish? I would occasionally e-mail my thoughts on God and religion to her. I probably overdid my advice and concern, and it didn't seem to take. I was always convinced of her goodness and innate spirituality, but it was not manifested in traditional church attendance.

Two years in the Peace Corps and two state-side jobs later, she e-mailed me one morning with a question: "Should you wipe the ashes off your forehead after you receive them or just leave them there?" I quickly typed back something like, "Well, there are two schools of thought on this. One is that the ashes are a witness to what you believe and you should not be ashamed of it. The other is that you should not parade your prayer or penances before others but rather go about these things quietly. So, I think either is appropriate. Why do you ask?" "Well, I've been thinking about how it is good to get into the rhythm of periodically assessing my life and asking forgiveness. It occurred to me that that's what Ash Wednesday is about, so I decided to get ashes and am looking around for a good parish."

QUESTIONS FOR REFLECTION
1. Which virtue do you find easiest?
2. Which do you find most difficult? Why?
3. Which virtue do you think you can commit to working on in the future? What steps will you take to practice this virtue?

Let Us Pray
For the strength and patience to practice each virtue every day
with our children.
For the serenity to know what we can control and what we can't,
and the wisdom to know the difference.
We pray to the Lord.
Lord, hear our prayer.

: THOUGHTS TO KEEP IN MIND :

Trust yourself, and trust in God.

Forgive others. Forgive yourself.

CHAPTER ONE

LIFE AFTER HIGH SCHOOL, COLLEGE, OR WHATEVER

• Key Virtues: Silence of words, Imagination, and Restraint •

YOU HAVE YOUR CAR BACK and perhaps a free bedroom to divvy up among other kids or make into an office. It's exciting to see your child go off to college, but it's also a tough transition because now you get to worry from afar. Of course, some young adults choose to grace their parent's home during the college years, and that brings its own blessings and challenges. Others don't choose college at all. They may go straight into the job market, spend time exploring the world, or seem just to vegetate while they wait for a lucrative (and easy) job offer from the NBA, "American Idol," or Microsoft.

Regardless, this is not only a transition for your child but also one for you. And, as with most transitions, this time will bring you both joy and heartache. You can figure it all out by yourself, but you don't have to. Other parents have walked similar paths and survived. So will you.

Although this book isn't solely about your enduring role of mentoring your child in faith, it's faith that has supported many parents during times of transition and crisis. The irony of your love and concern for your children during these times is that as much as you think your job is to influence *them*, the reality is that most of your work will be internal. You'll grow in your own spirituality as you understand, ever more deeply, the prophecy of Simeon to Mary: "And a sword will pierce your soul too" (Luke 2:35).

53

Realize also that, although one of the concerns many parents have as a child enters adulthood hovers around church attendance, "keeping the faith" is bigger than just going to church, synagogue, or mosque. Keeping the faith also has to do with your child internalizing values that you have tried to instill over the last eighteen-plus years, such as the importance of:

- a solid work ethic
- a healthy lifestyle
- self-respect and respect for others
- compassion and concern for others
- dedication, loyalty, and love toward family and others

Be grateful as you see your young adult grow in any of these broader areas. Generally, these values lead to a larger concept of God and holiness. That said, let us start with the concern most parents identified in my surveys about faith: "My child no longer goes to church regularly." We'll take it chronologically.

IF YOUR YOUNG ADULT IS PREPARING TO LEAVE FOR COLLEGE
Both you and your young adult will have concerns. Yours may include, "Will my child eat well and stay healthy? Stay in contact with me? Spend money wisely? Drink too much or make other irresponsible choices?" And of course, "Will she still go to church?" Meanwhile, she may have different priorities: "Will I be able to do the work? Will I be able to find a comfortable group of friends?" There are unknowns for both of you, and this can be scary. She may be homesick for a short time. You may want to protect or rescue her for a lot longer time. After all, you've had eighteen years of practice! Habits are hard to break.

One of the main jobs for parents during this transition is to assist your young adult in making decisions without taking over. The biggest challenge in doing this is to do it with few words and little money, lest it sound like nagging or become a bailout. (See the virtue of "silence of words" for more on this.)

Now, however, I want to share one strategy best done when your young adult is on the brink of starting college. I call it "The Letter."

THE LETTER

The value of "The Letter" is that you can be concise and pick the best words, and your young adult can save it. Hopefully, this isn't the first time that you've communicated with him about alcohol use, sex, or faith, but it is perhaps your last best chance to make a point without nagging. The purpose of "The Letter" is to share crucial nuggets of your beliefs in writing, then to promise not to bring the issue(s) up again unless *he* wants to talk. You might present "The Letter" to him the night before he departs for college or tuck it in his toiletry bag. The following is just a sample. I encourage you to draft your own in your own words.

> *Dear _____,*
>
> *I want to talk to you about sex (or drinking, or church attendance, or _____) while you are at college. It may be that this conversation is totally unnecessary, since I trust your good judgment, but I am writing this because I know how persuasive friends, the media, and our culture can be.*
>
> *Although you know from past conversations how Dad* (or Mom, if Dad is writing the letter) *and I feel about sex and marriage, I am not sure we have ever talked with you in depth about* why. *I have chosen to write my thoughts since I know I can get long-winded. My promise to you is that I will only say these views once and not bring them up again unless* you *want to talk further. This is my way of launching you into the next stage of your life and letting go, since moral and faith decisions must now be your responsibility.*
>
> *There are many reasons commonly given today to refrain from being sexually active before marriage:*

- *Pregnancy (no method is 100% effective, save abstinence)*
- *AIDS and other STDs*
- *Religious teachings*

Valid as the above reasons are (and even though the resulting problems can really mess up your life), to me they are not adequate in themselves as the core reason. To me, the most convincing reason comes from my experience of marriage and the nature of sexual intimacy. Yes, sex is pleasurable, but it can also be hollow. Its meaning comes from being the ultimate expression of self-giving, vulnerability, and commitment to the person you love.

Yes, you can "love" many persons throughout life, but ideally, there is only one to whom you commit to bind your life forever in marriage. That is total *commitment and is worthy of the total gift of self to another.*

What happens when sex is used more casually? Even with people who love each other but perhaps are not yet ready for the exclusive and permanent commitment of marriage, premature intercourse can short-circuit a relationship from growing on other planes. Couples stop talking and exploring other dimensions of their personalities. Much growth in emotional and intellectual intimacy can be thwarted.

Obviously, I cannot be with you twenty-four hours a day, and so you will have to seek your own truth in this arena. I do not know if you have already been sexually active. Regardless, I ask you to weigh my values as you make difficult decisions in college. I also want you to know that as my child, I will love you no matter what, and I hope that you will feel comfortable coming to Dad (or Mom, if Dad is writing) *and me if you ever have any difficulties in this area.*
Love,
Mom (or Dad)

My husband, Jim, has also written letters to our young adults at various milestones. Either parent can send a similar or modified version (based on the sex of your child) of the following:

Dear_____,

My wish for you as you move from adolescence to adulthood is that you may have RESPECT:

For women (or men)*: Treat no woman* (man)*–your girlfriends* (boyfriends), *your classmates, your sister* (brother), *your mother* (father), *the lonely woman* (man) *on the bus, or the poor woman* (man) *begging on the sidewalk–as an object or a means to an end. Do not use people for your own advantage or pleasure. Consequently, don't ignore them either, if they seem to serve no purpose to you.*

For your own sexuality: Do not use sex as merely a form of recreation. Do not use your power to procreate until you have found the person you want to live with the rest of your life, and you are both willing to commit to each other for life.

For your talents: Do not squander them or neglect them. Use your talents to make this world a better place.

For the poor or powerless: As my child, you have lived a privileged life. Be grateful for the doors that open to you, but always remember that from those who have been given much, much will be expected. Those who have been given less than you have a right to your care. It is justice, not charity.

For yourself: Do what is right. Always remember that I love you.

Love,

Dad (or Mom)

Other Letting-go Rituals

Some creative parishes have developed a liturgical ritual for "sending off" young adults leaving for college, the military, or volunteer commitments. Petitions at a worship service can be a start, but find out if your own parish has, or might develop, a more extensive ritual (see Appendix B for a sample.) For a more home-style send-off, you might prepare a special meal. After the meal, ask everyone present to place a hand on the young adult about to leave and offer a blessing or hope for the future. If any of your children no longer reside at home, ask them to send a few words of wisdom to be shared at this time. *Family Prayer for Family Times,* by Kathleen O'Connell Chesto, also has a creative home ritual.

If Your Young Adult Is Already in College

I hope most of your young adult's life in college is filled with not only new knowledge, but also great friendships and exciting new adventures. Regardless of how well things are going most of the time, she's bound to experience some bumps along the way. You want to be available to love and support her, but that doesn't mean running her life, talking with her professors, or rescuing her from the negative consequences of an impetuous act.

One of our children was diagnosed with diabetes just before leaving for college seven hundred miles away. Another came down with mononucleosis as she started her sophomore year. Another walked at graduation but took two more years to finish a final paper. Another had Attention Deficit Disorder. One of them didn't pay attention to the notice to complete a financial aid renewal form until we got a bill for $30,000, due immediately. When appropriate, Jim and I alerted the school to medical or psychological concerns, but there was not much we could do when our daughter got mono and the health center said they couldn't talk with us unless our daughter signed a release since she was no longer a minor. These situations are tough. What's a parent to do?

Since college expenses often are at least in part borne by the parents, you still have some leverage with your young adult. But wield it lightly, lest any infraction be a cause for withdrawal of funds. The primary job of the college student is to apply himself to academic work, so if poor grades occur, you have grounds for the "finance talk." Risky behavior such as excessive drinking, missing classes, and so on jeopardize not only grades but also your child's life. You can't save your children from all the mistakes they will make, but you can point out the connection between risky behavior and flunking out. Your college student is probably still covered under your health insurance. That will cover medical expenses but not wear and tear on your heart, which always holds them close.

As undesirable as missing church might be to you as parent, faith cannot be bought. You can request that your daughter check out the campus ministry or Newman Center, but you can't enforce this request. This is a time when you must return her to God's hands, believing that God loves her at least as much as you do. Let God do the work—that is, God, campus ministry staff, friends, and time. Meanwhile, pray—a lot.

IF YOUR YOUNG ADULT CONTINUES TO LIVE AT HOME OR RETURNS HOME ON VACATION

Only some college students continue to live at home, but almost all return home for vacations. The main question that parents have while their college students are at home (again) is how, or if, rules should change now that your young adults are, well...adults. Curfews (probably not appropriate at the college-age level), chores, and household responsibilities are something you can negotiate together. But there are some issues that you may feel less likely to negotiate. Here are some suggestions to help navigate the uncharted waters of rearing of an adult child:

- Sexual behavior and alcohol use may not be monitored at college, but it's reasonable to expect that your young adult abide by house rules. After all, you still have legal liability for drug or alcohol accidents that happen in your home. The caveat to call you for a ride home if he has been drinking still stands (like it did during his adolesence), with no questions asked. It's more important that he doesn't kill himself or someone else.

• Faith cannot be legislated. Hopefully, your young adult will want to join you for religious services, but the days of requiring it are over. Instead, invite. Encourage, especially if there are younger children at home who want to emulate their older sibling and would put up a fuss about going if he didn't. If he's only home on vacation, you might take the approach to honor his freedom to attend or not but explain that even if he isn't actively practicing his faith at college, coming with you is an act of family solidarity, showing that he values family unity, at least on special occasions.

• Even if–or *especially* if–your college student isn't actively participating in organized religion, make an effort to engage her in discussions about what beliefs and values she holds dear. Cherish the good heart and generous spirit that you see growing in her. I hope you see it. If not, look a little deeper.

IF YOUR ADULT CHILD IS NOT COLLEGE BOUND AND NO LONGER LIVES AT HOME

There are many reasons that a young adult may not be college bound. Some reasons, such as working in a trade he loves or being in the military, make a lot of sense. Some reasons may be disappointing to you. Regardless, if your young adult no longer lives with you, go now to chapter two and then be ready to rewind to this chapter or fast forward to chapter five, since boomeranging young adults are quite normal.

CHOOSE YOUR BATTLES: SEXUAL ACTIVITY, DRUGS, ALCOHOL, CHURCH ATTENDANCE

One of the graces of parenthood is learning which battles are worth fighting and which to let slide. By the time your child is of college age, you should have plenty of experience in this department. But now the rules of engagement are changing, since she's no longer a minor and you have less knowledge of what she does and less control over her actions. As much as you would like her not to abuse alcohol or drugs, wait until marriage to have sex, go to church every week, change her sheets weekly, and keep a neat room, you really don't have much power over these decisions. So don't waste your energy battling.

But, what about sex? Shouldn't you be very clear about your standards and expectations? Yes, but the time for clarity was long before your young adult left home. Many college students have told me that even though their parents didn't express it or to tell them directly, they knew their parents didn't approve of their being sexually active. Nevertheless, they engaged in sexual activity anyway, usually hiding it from their parents and often feeling guilty about their behavior. This situation distanced the young adults from their parents and their church. This doesn't make sex outside of marriage acceptable, but it tells me that never acknowledging such behavior is not a successful strategy. But, neither is arguing about it or demanding a child refrain from it. In fact, many young adults told me that they later regretted their sexual promiscuity but didn't think they would have listened if their parents had told them not to have sex. They said they had to learn the hard way. Our culture has a strong pull on young adults, and we can't protect them from every mistake.

The real battle will be with *you*—training yourself to stay out of the fray unless it's illegal, a matter of life and death, or harmful to a third party. Save your energy to pick up the pieces when your young adult's mistakes catch up with him. Like the father in the parable of the prodigal son, it will hurt to let your young adult make reckless decisions, but you must be ready to welcome him back when he comes home. It's hard to do this if you're still battling with him over who is right. Keep looking for his goodness and talents.

. . . . .

IN THEIR OWN WORDS: WHAT PARENTS LIKE YOU AND YOUNG ADULTS ARE SAYING ABOUT THIS PERIOD OF TRANSITION

Upon Returning Home/Visiting Home During College

"We've noticed that when many of our young adults returned home during college vacations or after college, they often reverted to their 'pre-adult behavior' when visiting. They would be perfectly capable of taking care of themselves at school or work, but once in the home environment, they would leave dishes in the sink or wet towels in the bathroom. We determined what was worth bringing up for negotiation, but let a lot go because we were so happy they were home." (Kathy B., parent, Portland, Maine)

"I have very firm beliefs in my Catholic faith. I also have very firm beliefs in allowing my children to express their feelings and opinions. They have a right to that, but they do not have a right to live immorally under my roof when I am supporting them financially. I never suppressed my children's need or want to express themselves unless it was immoral, unlawful, or infringed on the comfort or rights of others." (Sherry L., parent, Lake Charles, Lousiana)

On Church Attendance While Home

"In my late teens / early twenties, I just wanted to explore to see what else was out there. My mom was great, though. She challenged me (in a calm and non-confrontational way) and said, 'Before you go off looking for something else, why don't you take the time to really learn about what the Catholic faith teaches and has to offer, to really understand what you already have?'" (Amy A., young adult, Austin, Texas)

"We weren't at odds about faith but about practice. Both our kids were enticed by high-tech nondenominational megachurches, though they didn't fall prey to cheap theology. What made them susceptible was the lack of energy in our parish and the local Catholic campus ministry and the high energy and hospitality of the megachurches. For both our kids, the Eucharist called them back to practicing their Catholic faith, though they still would love more energy in the liturgies." (Andrew, L., parent, Chicago, Illinois)

"Regarding Mass attendance, we agreed on several changes after the kids moved away from home. While living at home, Mass attendance was a requirement. After moving to college, it was not expected every Sunday, but we asked them out of respect for us to join us when they could. The oldest asked if he committed to a volunteer organization and used his time for faith works, could he be excused from church on Sundays. I think it is important to let them explore and find their own faith and not just live out yours." (Nancy K., parent, Muskegon, Michigan)

Exploring Faith
"Our son attended a Jesuit high school and made a five-week service trip to Peru one summer with them. That was a life-changing experience that consolidated many of his religious beliefs and opened his eyes to many things.... His high school and service experiences brought Jesus' teachings to the foreground and put weekly Mass attendance in its rightful context, as one (but not the only) expression of faith and community. He now attends a private university where many of the professors and students identify as atheist. I think this was a surprise to him, but it hasn't shaken him beyond his ability to cope because he did some of the work on his own faith development before he got to college.

He now lives with eight other guys, most of them Hindu, and he has a profound appreciation for diversity. He took a world religions course in high school and read many of the great books of other religions, so he had some knowledge beforehand. It's exciting, not threatening, for me to see his curiousity about other religions." (Mary Kay F., parent, Crescent Springs, Kentucky)

QUESTIONS FOR REFLECTION

1. Which virtues seem most relevant to you at this stage of parenting? Consider especially silence of words, imagination, and restraint.
2. When was a time that you bit your tongue when you wanted to criticize or give unsolicited advice to your young adult? Can't remember? Maybe this is one virtue (the virtue of silence) to start working on.
3. When have you struggled with your faith? Is there anything about the church you attend that you think needs reform or improving? Does your young adult know not only of your belief but also of your struggles?
4. Do you know the pop culture, songs, words, technology of youth? Ask your young adult to share some of her favorites with you.
5. What form of prayer do you find most meaningful and satisfying?

Let Us Pray

For young adults who are genuinely seeking God, no matter what form it may take. May God guide them, and may we be patient with God's work.

For ourselves that we have the wisdom to recognize when to speak and when to keep silent.

We pray to the Lord.

Lord, hear our prayer.

: THOUGHTS TO KEEP IN MIND :

Return your young adult to God's hands.

Share your faith struggles, not just your certainty.

Your young adults will always be your children, but you
are no longer responsible for them.

CHAPTER TWO

THE SINGLE LIFE—FOR A WHILE OR FOREVER

• Key Virtues: Ingenuity, Mindfulness of Emotions, and Listening •

SO YOUR YOUNG ADULT IS now living independently–mostly. You no longer carry her on your auto insurance, and her debts are her own. Sure, you may still help with car-buying or repair decisions, you may recycle furniture from your home to her apartment, or you may invite her for Sunday dinner. But for the most part, your young adult is now blessedly on her own. Of course, helping each other out goes both ways, as she may become your unpaid tech support for your home computer or the first person you call when you need something heavy moved. Family is like that, isn't it? You can impose on family members more readily than others because of the deep bond you share.

Before we look at the challenges of relating to young adults during their time of living independently, let me remind you of the joys of having a young adult by sharing several stories of how the tables often get turned on us. For example, although none of our young adults has ever worked professionally as travel agents, all of them have actually performed that role for us as we visited them in different parts of our country and the world. Brian, the oldest, was the first. Soon after college, he participated in a volunteer program in Indonesia. Later, he interned in India for a master's degree in international policy. He looked on both of these experiences as furthering his education. We saw his, and all our children's, international placements as opportunities for us to see and understand the world, its people, and its various religions.

Having adult children is also like having fashion stylists on hand. My daughter, Heidi, has served as my very own fashion consultant since her high school years and even more so since she has become more sophisticated in her tastes. She updated my wardrobe with a surprise gift from a store I would have never frequented without her suggestion, and I now have a favorite outfit thanks to her—and an updated "not 1980s" wardrobe for speaking engagements and professional meetings.

My tech-savvy son Dacian has stepped in as my on-call support when *anything* technological goes wrong at home. We can also count on him to entertain us and offer mental stimulation whenever we settle in for a serious game of Settlers of Catan.

My youngest son, Aaron, is our on-call singer and hiking support. When Aaron did volunteer work in Singapore for a couple years, we decided to do a side trip together to Thailand, which involved a two-day trek to visit a hill tribe. On the way up the mountain with no switchbacks, I got slower and slower. Aaron eventually fell back to walk with me and started softly singing "The Girl from Ipanema"—in Portuguese. It brought tears to my eyes and comfort to my feet as I remembered singing that song to Aaron when he was ten years old and we were taking a twenty-mile hike—probably too long for a ten-year-old—in New Mexico. As a way to keep his mind off the time and his spirits up, we sang this song over and over, learning new verses from our Brazilian exchange student, André, who was with us.

I am not sure if Aaron was conscious of the connection, but for me it was a powerful example of role reversal and grace.

These stories illustrate the rewards of raising young adults. It's natural to be pleased when our children follow our path, look like us, or make us proud. That's the easy part of parenting. The spiritual challenge of parenthood, however, is to love our children unconditionally, just as God loves them. That means to love them with equal (or perhaps more) strength when they do things that we don't approve of or that disappoint us. We must remember the obvious: We are not our children! Our success as a parent does not depend on their success. Resist the urge to take credit for your young adult's successes, lest you also take the blame for his mistakes. (Well, OK, you can brag to the grandparents and closest friends, but don't get carried away with it.)

Within this dance of give and take, pride and concern, issues upon which you disagree are bound to crop up. Some issues are trivial, such as "Are the Cincinnati Bengals (where you live) or the Washington Redskins (where he lives) the better team?" "Is gray really her most flattering color?" Other issues, such as politics, lifestyle, morals, and, yes, faith, are much more fundamental. This is stressful to some parents, while others have learned to accept the differences. The heart of this book is to help you understand how and when to advise and when to keep our advice to yourself, when to intervene and when to step back, when to talk and when to shut up. Managing this delicate balance is an art. Wise parents gradually learn to love their young adults unconditionally, even when experience tells them there might be danger or unhappiness ahead. As always, a prudent mentor must choose which battles to fight.

Choose Your Battles: Cohabitation

There are many battles that a parent of a young adult should decide *not* to fight, and the number increases as your child gets older. If he goes to church regularly, rejoice that he has found a spiritual home; don't fight it if it is not *your* home. Many parents would love to trade places with you. Perhaps you're concerned that he doesn't have any regular church affiliation. That may be a sadness for you, but focus on the positive. Perhaps he leads a life of generous service and maintains his home-grown values. A nagging war between you will only wear you both down and result in a stalemate or worse–resentment.

Serious physical or moral lapses that are life-threatening or harm others, however, warrant intervention. When it's time to intervene, it's also time to bring in experts—a counselor, other family members, and the Holy Spirit. (See chapter five for more on interventions in crises such as addictions, unplanned pregnancy, and mental illness.)

Cohabitation

The battles that many parents in my surveys faced during their young adult's single life centered around cohabitation. To fight or not to fight, that is the question. The answer is: It depends. Research shows that, if cohabiting couples do marry, they have a 46 percent higher divorce rate than couples who don't cohabit before marriage. (For more information, read "Should We Live Together," David Popenoe and Barbara Dafoe Whithead.) This doesn't include couples who were already engaged or otherwise committed to marry each other when they first cohabited. It seems to make a difference if the couple had already decided to marry as opposed to using the cohabitation experience as a way to decide, or simply sliding into marriage because it would be too uncomfortable to break up.

Not only does living together without a previous commitment or engagement before marriage increase the risk of divorce, it also increases the risk of domestic violence for women and the risk of physical and sexual abuse for children. In addition, unmarried couples have lower levels of happiness and well-being than married couples. (For more, see *The National Marriage Project*, www.virginia. edu/marriageproject.) These statistics do not impute a causal relationship or that all cohabiting couples will divorce, but it does alert us that there is something about the practice of cohabiting that puts couples at higher risk.

Now, just because you know the facts does not mean you should beat your young adult over the head with them. The vast majority of young adults (and also many parents) believe that cohabitation is a natural and helpful step toward making a lasting commitment in marriage, and it is counterintuitive to suggest otherwise. You could refer them to the research in *Sex Without Strings, Relationships Without Rings* or *Should We Live Together*. For many young adults, however, suggesting books would feel like preaching, and they would resent it.

A more indirect, and perhaps more effective, approach is to tell your young adult that you like her partner (if you do) and ask what is holding her back from making the decision to marry. It may simply be money, or it may be that there is some doubt about whether this is the right person. If it is the latter, voicing that doubt can help her recognize that she isn't ready for the commitment that sexual bonding implies. (If you don't like the partner, see chapter three on marriage.) If you cohabited before marriage, reflect aloud on the pros and cons of your own experience. Maybe cohabitation was helpful to you, or maybe you learned some cautions that would be worth sharing.

The practical side of cohabitation that many parents in my surveys addressed is what to do when the couple comes to visit you. Most parents responded that they warmly welcome their young adult's significant other, don't make a fuss about it, and put them in separate bedrooms. Usually nothing more is said. The parents uphold their value in their own home but do not impose it upon others.

What about the morality of cohabitation? Isn't it important to impress upon our children that premarital sex (which cohabitation presumes) is against most religious mores? The answer is yes, of course, most religions don't condone premarital sex or cohabitation. However, that's not the point. I in no way want to flaunt the teaching of any religion, but by the time your child is a young adult, it's too late to preach that line. For one, unless your family has been living in a cave, he well knows that mainline religions oppose cohabitation. He's probably well aware of your own position on it. Trying to make the point now is overkill and will most likely foster resentment. Young adults don't usually respond favorably to moral arguments based on "because the church teaches," just as they no longer find it persuasive to do what you say "because I said so." Since grace builds on nature, they would more likely be swayed by scientific research that indicates increased risk to a happy future marriage. The important thing is to maintain a loving relationship with your young adult and not short-circuit communication with sermons.

Support your child's independence. How does a parent help out without taking over or advise without furthering dependence? It's often a tough call and takes seeing beyond the usual worldly solutions. For example, will lending your son money get him out of a temporary tight spot so he can pick himself up and recover, or will bailing him out stifle his ability to be responsible? Will welcoming him home when he needs your emotional and physical support after a failed relationship be what is needed to help him get back on his feet, or will he become a long-term resident? The key question about whether and how much to help is: Will this action empower my child to become more independent, or will it foster continuing dependence on me?

Decisions like these take concentration as you think through the ramifications of temporary help versus long-term codependence. Each situation is different, just as each child is different. Keeping yourself centered as you try to think of creative solutions often starts with a trip back to your own core beliefs. What about your faith is really essential to you? Can you put it into one sentence? When have you felt the presence of God? The more you deepen your own faith and grow in understanding of how everything in the universe is connected, the easier it will be to recognize that your young adult's journey may be winding, but that doesn't mean she is lost. It is just a different path that, with grace, will lead her to the same God who loves us all.

Stretch your own faith. Just as your young adult is growing in experience (and hopefully wisdom), so should you. This means there might be parts of your life, especially your spiritual life, that you have taken for granted. Andrew and Terri Lyke of Chicago tell the story of how they had been going to the same parish for years. It wasn't a bad parish, but it also wasn't challenging them and inspiring them to new depths of faith. As Andrew explains, "We have struggled with our participation in our parish of more than twenty years. We joined a new parish that was less trapped in the suburban, middle-class bubble. We now have a parish that teaches and lives Catholic social teaching and celebrates the Eucharist with great energy. It feels refreshing."

Consider that this time of transition, in which you continue to let go of feeling responsible for your young adult's life, may be the very time in which you take a new responsibility for your own growth in faith. Is God calling you to try a new role in your faith community, to let go of a previous notion of how God works in your life, or to update your knowledge about your faith?

. . . . .

In Their Own Words: What Parents Like You and Young Adults Are Saying About This Period of Transition

Boomerang Young Adults
"Randy dropped out of college senior year, partially because he was hooked on the video game, World of Warcraft. When he came back home to live, he often would stay up late on the computer. Eventually, I set a boundary since he didn't seem to be able to do it for himself. I said, "You can't be on the computer after midnight in my house." He complained and said, "You've got to be joking. I don't believe this." but I heard him get ready for bed just a few minutes later! It's

hard to know how much motherly direction to give to a 24-year-old, but sharing a home again required it." (M.J.M., parent, Tallahassee, Florida)

"We invited our daughter and son-in-law to live with us when they were in temporary financial straits. Because they had already established a household, it was a challenge to all of us to integrate all our 'stuff.' Furniture, household supplies, and eating habits did not always mesh, but we compromised as adults do. We even made a car plan. We parents would always park our two cars behind each other so that one lane would be available for their car. That way we weren't always blocking each other in." (Steve B., parent, Portland, Maine)

Sex and Cohabitation

"My sons know my beliefs in certain things are strong and some are not flexible. I let them know where I stood on premarital sex and cohabitation. When they visited our house with their girlfriends, separate rooms were provided and expected. All understood and abided by the 'house rules.' When a pregnancy preceded marriage, it took great strength to support them and their choice, but by doing so we have maintained very close relationships with them." (Beverly H., parent, Madison, Wisconsin)

"We also try to be true to our own values. One cohabiting son and fiancée came for Christmas when his younger brothers were in high school. He asked where he and his fiancée would sleep. We said in separate bedrooms and explained why. He grinned and said, 'I figured you'd say that. Just wanted to check!'" (W.H., parent, Houston, Texas)

Church Attendance

"I did not attend church during my four years of college since mom was not there to push me to go. Then I decided to return to church on my own. Once I realized I was going to church for my own spiritual growth, and not because it was important to mom, my faith was able to blossom." (B. Kuhn, young adult, Austin, Texas)

"The point of conflict came when my parents started demanding that I go to church. A couple of years after hassling me, I came back into my faith. It was then I could finally say that it was *my* faith, not the faith my parents imposed on me." (Anonymous young adult)

Employment/Income

"It's been hard to watch our young adults struggle with meager incomes or unemployment. It's tempting to want to rescue them. So much depends on the situation. If one of our three kids needed money for a health reason, something directly related to employment, or to further their education, we lent them money. If they didn't have the money to pay their phone bill or for the Internet, we let them learn the hard way." (Kathy M., parent, St. Louis, Missouri)

QUESTIONS FOR REFLECTION

1. Which virtues seem most relevant to you at this stage of parenting? Consider especially ingenuity, mindfulness of emotions, and listening. Which comes easiest, Which is hardest? Why?
2. With what life skill, insight, or new knowledge has your young adult helped you?
3. Although you and your young adult may agree on many issues, are there any areas of concern or fear you have that are bones of contention between you?

4. Whom do you consider wise parents who have young adults just a little older than yours? Are there any concerns that you would like to talk over with these parents?

Let Us Pray

For young adults who are seeking their place in the world. May they find satisfying work and friends who care.

For ourselves, that we observe well and listen attentively to others. Give us the creativity and calm we need to respond helpfully.

We pray to the Lord.

Lord, hear our prayer.

: THOUGHTS TO KEEP IN MIND :

You are not your children! Your success as a parent does not depend on their successes. Resist the urge to take credit for your young adult's successes, lest you also take the blame for their mistakes.

When you want to help out, ask yourself: Will this action empower my child to become more independent, or will it foster continuing dependence on me?

Don't listen with your answer running.

As prayer deepens, it usually broadens and becomes less specific.

CHAPTER THREE

CHOOSING A MATE AND PLANNING A WEDDING

• Key Virtues: Giving Counsel, Renewal of Resolutions,
and Peacemaking •

JACINTA AND MARK WERE ENGAGED. Jacinta's parents were concerned because they didn't see in Mark the capacity to love generously. Their dilemma was whether to share their misgivings with Jacinta. Would it drive her to defend Mark and alienate the prospective son-in-law? They decided to share their concern with Jacinta while reiterating that they trusted her judgment and would welcome Mark wholeheartedly into the family if this was her choice. They knew Jacinta and Mark would be attending a reputable marriage preparation program, so they prayed and said no more. During the Engaged Encounter, Jacinta observed how other couples treated each other and that, by comparison, Mark acted like a spoiled teenager. She decided to break off the engagement. It was hard, but her parent's words helped her to be open to this possibility and to make the decision herself.

A discussion of marriage such as the one above must begin before any wedding or, preferably, before even the engagement. I hope you find that you really like the man or woman with whom your young adult appears to be getting serious. Still, there are bound to be times leading up to the wedding and afterward when you see things differently. Generally, these are relatively minor and can be handled by the overall rule of thumb: Intervene as little as possible, and trust your young adult's good judgment.

CHOOSE YOUR BATTLES: YOUR YOUNG ADULT'S SPOUSE, WEDDING, AND FAITH

The most common potential issues that you might face surrounding marriage are choice of spouse, wedding plans, and, in the faith department, whether this marriage will support or weaken your young adult's faith.

Choice of Spouse

If you're pleased with your future in-law, great! The only caution here is that it is rare but possible to love your fiance(é) too much. Make sure that he doesn't replace your own child's place in your heart. Maybe you hope that this new person will finally refine your daughter into a respectable, reliable person. You might find yourself praising and weighing the views of the fiancé more than your own child's. Be sure to keep that in check, and you can happily move on to wedding plans.

If, however, you're at the other extreme–you feel strongly that your young adult's current love would be a disastrous choice–be aware that it's still risky for you to criticize the partner. Often, this kind of criticism will drive him more quickly into the arms of the condemned. You can, however, ask questions, such as, "How does it make you feel when Heather embarrasses you in public?" "Does her drinking cause you to worry, or do you think she has control over it?" If it's clear to friends and other relatives who know and love your son that this particular marriage would cause grief, it may be time to enlist them to share their concerns. Always end any intervention with the assurance that if he does marry his fiancée, you will fully accept the choice and welcome her into the family. Once the engagement is official, it's time to move from prevention mode into support mode. This is the time to support the marriage and help your child make it work.

Giving advice to adults of any age is risky. Marriage advice can be especially sensitive since it also involves your child's fiance(é) or spouse. Two strategies that can help are:

Give options. "Well, the choices I see are to suck it up and ignore your husband's criticisms, talk with him frankly but lovingly about your feelings, attend a marriage enrichment event, talk with a counselor, or separate. Are there other options you can think of?"

You might follow it with sharing how you have handled a similar problem. The wording should be something like, "Here's what worked (or didn't work) for me," rather than, "Here's what I think you should do." Make it clear that any advice you offer is a suggestion, not a command.

Give information that the young adult may not be aware of. There are ways of giving counsel without it sounding like advice. The secret is to focus on sharing information that your young adult may not be aware of. What she does with the information is up to her. For example, the Catholic church and most mainstream religions in the United States require some form of marriage preparation for couples as they approach marriage. Even if the couple is not affiliated with any organized religion, it's still wise to attend a marriage preparation program. The Catholic church has perhaps the most developed programs of marriage preparation, with many options from which to choose. Your young adult may not be aware of the range of options and be inclined to just pick the cheapest or quickest. Some parents offer to pay for a marriage preparation program as an engagement present for the marrying couple.

Similarly, the engaged couple may not be aware of how much money you can afford to spend on the wedding. That is information you should share if the couple is expecting you to pay for some or all of the wedding. As they get started in their married lives, they may or may not be experienced in financial matters, home maintenance, and the like. It's fine to share information about such things, as long as it is presented sensitively, and as options to consider, not advice that you expect the couple to follow.

After reflection and exercising restraint, if you have a bone that you really must pick with your young adult, it's always wise and respectful to do it privately so as not to cause public embarrassment (Matthew 18:15). Finally, when dealing with in-law issues, remember counselor Bill Dougherty's advice: "Blood should argue with blood."

Wedding Planning

There are so many details related to planning a wedding that there are also grounds for many battles. It's not really worth fighting any of these battles, even if you're paying for the wedding. You can let your preferences be known, but your job is to support the couple in this momentous step. In other words, you have the fundamental job of raising your young adult to be a mature life partner. This role should be honored. In terms of wedding decisions, however, you are consultants and background beige.

Traditionally, the parents of the bride pay for the wedding and reception, while the parents of the groom pay for the rehearsal dinner. Such a "gift" is nice, but it's entirely appropriate to set a limit on what you can afford—even if it is nothing at all. Sometimes the tension is between the future in-laws, with one family expecting a fancier affair than the other. Hold tight to your limits and remember that weddings are a celebration of love—not an occasion to impress, settle past grudges, or prove your status in society. Of course, many couples marry later and have accumulated enough money to pay for much or all of the wedding themselves. In that case, support their independence, and offer a nice wedding gift.

Weddings and Faith

Engaged Encounter reminds couples, "A wedding is a day. A marriage is a lifetime." It's easy to forget this when our culture and advertisers put so much emphasis on the wedding day itself. Although I've already stated that parents should be consultants, not decision-makers, there are still some concerns and expectations that parents often carry about the wedding itself. While you may feel that the religion your young adult chooses to practice or not practice is up to her, you may still feel emotionally attached to the couple's getting married in your church. Or, you may feel nostalgically attached to the tradition of the father of the bride walking his daughter down the aisle and giving her away. These potential "battles" are best left to the priest, minister, rabbi, or imam to handle with the wedding couple.

For your own background, however, let me address the most common sensitive concerns that marriage ministers face and the current thinking about these concerns. Most ministers consider it disingenuous for a couple who have no explicit faith, nor intention to return to the practice of their faith, to use the church building to please their parents or to provide a beautiful setting. This can be balanced by the understanding that life transitions such as marriage are opportunities to reconnect with a faith that has been dormant. A wise minister will use this occasion to welcome young adults home and, it is to be hoped, inspire them to rediscover the faith they have been missing.

On the issue of walking the bride down the aisle, many of us support the tradition to have the father of the bride escort her to the groom and then "give her away," a practice that originated when daughters were considered property over which men had control. However, since most religions consider marriage to be a free and mutual commitment of equals, the symbolic gesture of handing one human over to another contradicts the meaning of the vows. This is particularly the case with the Catholic sacrament of marriage. Many couples resolve this by having both sets of parents walk them down the aisle as a symbol of the joining of two families. Alternatively, the bride and groom may walk themselves down the aisle and find another way to honor their parents. This is not your battle. Be supportive of whatever the couple works out with the person who presides at the ceremony.

Another wedding concern for some Catholic parents is the desire for the couple to be married "in the church." This often means more than just being married in a Catholic church building; it carries the connotation of being married Catholic. If both bride and groom are practicing Catholics, this is not an issue. If one partner is Christian but not Catholic, however, the couple sometimes wants to get married in the church building of the Protestant partner. Assuming the dispensation has been granted, the Catholic church fully recognizes this as a sacramental Catholic marriage. Likewise, the couple may get married in the Catholic church building but not have a Mass. This does not in any way lessen the sacredness and import of the sacrament but rather is an effort for the Catholic community to be hospitable to non-Catholics who are present, especially the non-Catholic spouse. Since marriage is a sacrament of unity, it might seem divisive to have part of the Mass (Communion) in which only one spouse partakes. Let the person who is responsible for your young adult's marriage preparation deal with these issues.

Sometimes a Catholic wedding may be complicated by the fact that one partner is divorced. While there are many misunderstandings about the need for a divorced person to seek an annulment to be free to enter a sacramental marriage, it is best to let the priest or deacon who coordinates the couple's marriage preparation deal with this in a pastoral manner. If requested, the parents' role is to guide the couple to competent and pastoral ministers. In addition to issues of the sacramentality of the first marriage, a marriage preparation program for couples entering a second marriage will help the couple sort through any issues that may linger from the first marriage. If your young adult is committed to both his faith and his beloved, encourage him to see the resources the church offers as an investment in a happy future, rather than hoops to jump through.

Finally, the couple may have no interest in getting married in a religious ceremony. As disappointing as this might be for parents who hold faith dear, you should respect the couple for not being hypocrites. It's the developmental job of young adults to come into their own. This often means separating from the faith of their childhood and trying on other ways, even if the other ways are over a vast period of what appears to be nothing. They may return to some form of organized religion later, or they may pursue a more generalized spirituality. You may not like it, but you cannot force-feed faith. Concentrate on developing a loving relationship with the couple.

. . . . .

IN THEIR OWN WORDS: WHAT PARENTS LIKE YOU AND YOUNG ADULTS ARE SAYING ABOUT THIS PERIOD OF TRANSITION

Choice of Spouse
"When I was fearful for the success of our children's decision to marry, my faith mentor assured me that my support of my children would make a difference in their success. That realization brought about a change in outlook, from fear and concern to giving me hope and a sense of control in what seemed a most difficult situation." (Beverly, H., parent, Madison, Wisconsin)

Interreligious Marriages
"I was at odds with my parents when I converted to Catholicism and was married in a traditional Catholic Mass. My parents could not understand why it would be important for me to have the same faith as my husband and our children. They had a lot of misunderstanding surrounding the Catholic faith." (M. G., young adult, Cincinnati, Ohio)

"When my oldest began to discover the depth of resistance to faith his girlfriend had, he thought he could just avoid the issue. We encouraged him to reach out to a man from the parish who had married a nonbeliever and raised his kids in faith alone. After sixteen years of modeling and prayer, his wife came to be received into the church. He gave my son the soundest advice: 'You can only marry a nonbeliever if you are OK praying every day for a person who will not be praying for you.' My son really thought he would be OK being the faith-centered person in the relationship. Eventually the relationship ended, not specifically because of a faith argument, but about what they believed marriage to be. He simply knew he would not marry a woman who did not think that sacrificial love was part of the equation." (Mary B., parent, Minneapolis, Minnesota)

QUESTIONS FOR REFLECTION

1. Which virtues seem most relevant to you at this stage of parenting? Consider especially giving counsel, renewal of resolutions, and wisdom. Which comes easiest to you? Which is hardest? Why?

2. If you're married, how do you keep your own marriage fresh? If you're not married, who are the friends who support you in your life commitments?

3. If you could only give your married child one piece of advice, what would it be? Is this something you should keep to yourself, or would it be welcome advice?

4. What issue most tempts you to want to intervene in your young adult's life? If, after prayer and reflection, you deem that saying something is warranted, how could you do it in a way that would build independence?

5. Have you ever sought counseling yourself? Have others sought advice from you? How has this experience been humbling or useful?

Let Us Pray

For young adults who are seeking someone
with whom to share their life.

For ourselves, that we grow in faithfulness to
our commitments and our word.

We pray to the Lord.

Lord, hear our prayer.

: THOUGHTS TO KEEP IN MIND :

If your young adult directly asks for advice, respond as you would to a peer or good friend.

One exception to the "wait until you're asked" rule is when there is life-threatening danger to your young adult, her spouse, or her children.

CHAPTER FOUR

THEIR CHILD(REN) AND YOUR
GRANDCHILD(REN)

• Key Virtues: Joy, Balancing Service and Energy,
and Self-sacrifice •

BEFORE I HAD ANY GRANDCHILDREN, I continually was amazed at how
all the grandparents I encountered were over-the-top in love with
their grandchildren. They assured me that I would feel the same way
when we had grandchildren of our own. If you are reading this chapter, you probably already know this. No matter what differences you
may have with your own children about how to raise the grandchildren, or mixed feelings you may have had if a grandchild was con-
ceived before marriage, still, your love for this tiny human being is
overwhelming. Now that Jim and I have the smartest, most beautiful
granddaughter on this planet who is destined to be president of the
world, I understand.

The transition to grandparenthood is not as great as the transition
to parenthood, but the natural inclination from having raised kids
for more than eighteen years is to give advice. As understandable as
this is, I will repeat: The older your offspring, the less advice you
should give–unless it's requested. You may worry and pray as much
as you like. The statute of limitations never runs out on worrying or
praying.

The temptation to ignore this advice on not advising, however, is
powerful. If you successfully cultivated the virtue of restraint, however, during your child's college years, his years of independence,
and his wedding and early married days, now may be the time when

that restraint bears fruit, because for many young adults, the birth of a first child is a gateway to a reexamination of faith. As parents become awed by the responsibility they have for a new life, their thoughts naturally turn to the ultimate questions of life and values. Although this doesn't always happen, the wise grandparent waits to see how God might work in the hearts of the new parents and respects God's ways and timing.

CHOOSE YOUR BATTLES: DISCIPLINING, SETTING BOUNDARIES, COPING WITH UNPLANNED PREGNANCIES, STEP-GRANDPARENTING, AND RELIGIOUS UPBRINGING OF GRANDCHILDREN

Parent-grandparent disagreements that arise during this stage often relate to child discipline, setting boundaries, and, in the realm of faith, whether the child will be baptized and raised in the religion of the grandparents.

Disciplining Grandchildren

This is an easy decision: Don't interfere. The only exception is when there's a situation of neglect or abuse of a child. Even if you have a doctorate in child development, the parent, not the grandparent, must be the disciplinarian (unless of course, the grandparent has custody of the child , or if the grandparent is a major caretaker for an extended period of time). The grandparent's role is to support the young parents as the primary disciplinarians. In fact, this is one of the joys of grandparenting: You don't have to be the punisher. Even if you disagree with the leniency or strictness of the parents, support their decisions. When the grandkids visit you, it's acceptable to pamper them a bit–after all, that's the prerogative of a grandparent. Just make sure you honor the parents' directions and wishes.

Setting Boundaries

Just as the new parents will need to set boundaries on how much help and advice they want from you, you'll need to figure out what your boundaries are. Perhaps the new parents live out of town, and your time with them and your grandchild will be limited by geography. You may want more frequent contact, which just isn't practical. On the other hand, the new parents may live nearby and regard you as convenient and trusted babysitters. Maybe you're thrilled with this prospect; maybe you're not. You may want to be generous in helping with childcare, but you may need to weigh current jobs, volunteer commitments, and physical ability and energy levels (think lifting, carrying, and running after) before committing yourself. Your memories of early childhood care may have faded!

Coping With Unplanned Pregnancies

In this situation, you continue to love your child and begin the challenging task of supporting him or her and his or her child without supplanting him or her as parent. Does this mean you invite the new family to live with you? Maybe, maybe not. I know of many generous grandparents who have risen to this challenge, put retirement from parenting on hold, and reentered the world of diapers and semipermanent childcare. As admirable as this sacrifice is, it's important to jointly discern boundaries and an exit plan. Is your single-parent child going to date or continue to pursue recreational activities, assuming that you'll be a ready babysitter? If you disagree on discipline, whose way will hold sway if you're the one who spends the most time with the child? Is your home a temporary place of respite while your son or daughter pursues educational goals or job advancement that will empower her to set up her own household in a year or two? These are questions that are best addressed beforehand as part of the agreement you make in preparation for opening your home to your extended family.

Step-Grandparenting

If your young adult becomes an instant stepparent through marriage, you become an instant grandparent. The challenge is to treat all grandchildren—biological, adoptive, or step—with equal regard and attention. After all, this is the way God regards all children—equally deserving of unconditional love. Sometimes this is easy, sometimes it's harder because you've known the biological children longer or feel more physically connected to your own genes. You may not always *feel* equally attached to each grandchild, but you must strive to *treat* them all similarly. Of course, the opposite scenario sometimes happens, in which stepchildren, by virtue of having multiple sets of grandparents, get multiple presents on holidays to the point of overload and reverse discrimination. Take your lead from the children's parents as to what's needed.

Religious Upbringing of Grandchildren

If you and your young adult are on the same page in terms of the religious upbringing of your grandchildren, friction is unlikely. Your primary job will be to reinforce the religious training to which you're all committed. Grandparents are wonderful supports in this area, since they often can share religious devotions that might be lost to the modern parent but still appeal to young children, such as holy cards, blessings, devotions, and memorized prayers.

For those who don't have compatible religious practices, however, there may be tension. For many Christians, the first question revolves around infant baptism. It's not worth fighting over whether your grandchild should be baptized or go to church. These faith-related issues may be important to you, and it's natural for you to want to pass your faith on to your grandchildren. But unless the parents are active church-goers and they plan to follow up and reinforce an infant baptismal commitment, your actions of pouring the water and saying the formulaic baptismal words over the child are not the most important thing—faith is. Baptism is not magic. The ritual of baptism reflects the reality of faith. It reflects a commitment to the Christian faith and thus welcomes the baptized into the Christian community. Since an infant cannot consciously make that commitment, the parents and godparents voice the decision for the child

with the intention of raising the child to the point of personal acceptance. If at least one parent does not have that intention, it is not
likely that grandparents, godparents, or other well-meaning relatives will be able to adequately fill the gap.

Infant baptism presumes that the baby will be raised in the
Christian faith. Yes, some grandparents privately pour water on
their grandchild's head and "conditionally baptize" the child. This
reflects the faith and hope of the grandparents. More helpful than a
conditional baptism, however, would be for you as grandparents to
share the reality of your own faith with the grandchild as he grows
toward maturity. This might take the form of sharing stories of
saints, teaching him simple prayers, or talking about how God has
touched your life. Of course, you would want to be sensitive to the
parents' beliefs and not engage in proselytizing if it is clearly in
opposition to their wishes. Otherwise, you risk damaging your relationship with your own child and reducing your access to your
beloved grandchildren. Your presence as a loving, moral person in
their midst may be all that you can do, and it will be enough. Be
assured that God loves your grandchildren unconditionally and
would not abandon them.

If the parents are not opposed to your faith but just not actively
practicing it, you could offer to share with your grandchild some of
the religious practices you find meaningful. Young children often
have an innate appreciation for prayer and ritual and enjoy activities
such as learning the meaning behind religious symbols, taking a
church tour and learning the stories of the stained-glass windows, or
using a holy card as a bookmark. Some parents believe in waiting
until children are old enough to choose their own religion, although
this can be difficult if a child has no experience of any religion and,
therefore, can't make a knowledgeable choice.

. . . . .

IN THEIR OWN WORDS: WHAT PARENTS LIKE YOU AND YOUNG ADULTS ARE SAYING ABOUT THIS PERIOD OF TRANSITION

Baptism

"We are Roman Catholic, but our son and daughter-in-law did not have their daughter (now two) baptized. We discussed the situation and basically agreed to disagree. We don't agree with their decision, but respect it." (G.B., parent, Cincinnati, Ohio)

"Baptism of grandchildren is the issue that has been the most stressful. Eventually our first grandson was baptized after our child realized that she did believe and wanted the child to be baptized Catholic, even as her husband, raised a Catholic, was not sure in what he believed. We are called to love him as he searches out faith and its place in his life." (Peter E., parent, Fargo, North Dakota)

"Both my son and daughter and their spouses are good parents, and my grandchildren are being brought up with a lot of love and to respect other people. Somehow I believe that God is in charge and, to quote Julian of Norwich, 'All will be well.'" (Jean Mary T., parent, Front Royal, Virginia)

What a Difference a Child Makes

"I rediscovered my faith when I had my first child. By then my parents were completely out of the church and resisted, even mocked, my renewed faith. I now teach Sunday school and my parents still believe this is a phase somehow and that I will eventually come round to my senses." (Anne D., young adult, Lutherville, Maryland)

"My oldest daughter was not married in the church. We were honest with her about our concerns but acknowledged that as an adult she would make her own decisions. She told us they intended to rectify the situation in their own time and did, in fact, having their marriage blessed the same day they baptized their son." (Ann K., parent, San Antonio, Texas)

"It has been different with each son: The married sons are practicing Catholics, the single one's not. Wife and children made a difference. Prayer for each other seems to be a common thread that connects us, practicing or not." (W.H., parent, Houston, Texas)

"I see men much more interested in home and family than was the case in my generation. I see them being good daddies and engaged in the household with their wives. I see men and women being more thoughtful about how they raise children and when to have children. Many people are opting to marry later in life than my generation did and I believe that can add stability to families." (anonymous parent)

QUESTIONS FOR REFLECTION

1. Which virtues seem most relevant to you at this stage of parenting? Consider especially joy, balancing service and energy, and self-sacrifice. Which is easiest for you? Which is hardest? Why?
2. What differences do you notice between the way you raised your child and the way parents (especially your own young adults) are raising children today? What do you think is an improvement, and what is a loss?
3. What gives you the most joy about being a grandparent?
5. Sometimes it's difficult to recognize our own biases or self-righteousness. If you're brave enough, ask someone you trust if

PARENTING YOUR ADULT CHILD

you have any blind spots that might keep you from honoring all members of the human race, not just those who are like yourself.

Let Us Pray

For young adults who are extending their love for each other to create a new generation. May they be wise and generous parents.

For ourselves, that as much as we rejoice in the creation of new life, we accept our limitations. Help us, God, to find new ways of continuing to make a difference in the world according to our time and talents.

We pray to the Lord.

Lord, hear our prayer.

: THOUGHTS TO KEEP IN MIND :

The older your offspring, the less advice you should give, unless directly asked.

If your young adult has stepchildren beyond the age of infancy, reassure her that bonding takes time. Both of you should go slowly and not expect instant affection or loyalty.

CHAPTER FIVE

IF YOUR CHILD MARCHES TO THE BEAT OF
A DIFFERENT DRUMMER

• Key Virtues: Wisdom, Unconditional Love, and Forgiveness •

JAMES IS A RECOVERING DRUG addict. Despite his parents' vigorous efforts to help him in every way possible, he continued to resist, and it almost cost him his life. After twenty years of self-abuse, he decided to ask for God's help. What prompted this? Perhaps the unrelenting prayers of his mother and grandmother over the years. Perhaps desperation. Perhaps grace. Perhaps it was just his time. James credits God with turning his life around and keeping him clean, but he regrets the years wasted.

Not every story has a happy ending that we see in our lifetime, but as the angel said to Mary, "Nothing will be impossible with God" (Luke 1:37). What if your young adult has issues that are deeper or more complicated than just not wanting to go to church? What if you can't honestly say that you think she's a generous and healthy human being, and you have confidence in her values? What if she still feels that being a video game tester is the ideal career? What if you yourself feel that you made some serious mistakes in raising her and are feeling guilt ridden? Is it too late to turn this train around?

Welcome to reality. You are not alone. Every parent has a different story, just as each child is unique, but the company of others is helpful. The good news is that there are saints who trod this road. Remember St. Monica's wayward son, St. Augustine. Remember the many anonymous saints whom you've known personally, who have shed their share of tears and survived.

Most of this book is geared to parents whose children have taken the most commonly traveled path through college to marriage and parenthood. There are ample challenges even when no extraordinary circumstances present themselves. Yet there are also plenty of parents whose young adults march to the beat of a different drummer or who have made choices that require special attention. There are two broad categories of these special circumstances: *just different* and *crisis*. Perhaps one or more of your young adults fits into these categories.

WHEN YOUR ADULT CHILD IS "JUST DIFFERENT"
Did you know that Steve Jobs, cofounder of Apple, Inc., dropped out of college after just one semester? Or that billionaire financier Charles Schwab had a learning disability? Or that scores of famous, accomplished people were homosexuals? There is nothing "wrong" with these people or situations.

As a parent, it can be challenging when your young adult doesn't fit the established mold. Yet this isn't uncommon. Most neighborhoods have a sampling of boomerang young adults whose parents gladly give them a place to land between jobs or following a failed marriage. Do any of the following scenarios fit your young adult? He:

- didn't go directly to college after high school or hasn't identified a clear work or education path
- is gay
- is physically or mentally challenged
- returns home like a boomerang for extended periods between jobs, marriages, or relationships
- has divorced or had multiple divorces
- has had a child or children outside of marriage

Parents generally love these young adults unconditionally. Often, however, they fear how others will regard or treat them.

When Your Adult Child is in "Crisis"

Some young adults make decisions that impact their lives in more dramatic and potentially destructive ways. It might be a temporary crisis, such as dropping out of school, but often the crisis is so serious that it threatens their future and your relationship with them. Sometimes parents can see it coming, but more often we're blindsided and wringing our hands, wondering if we might have done something to prevent crises such as addictions, untreated mental illness, or antisocial or criminal behavior.

Young adults who face a crisis during these years often require a more active form of parenting (that is, more "hands on," frequent monitoring, and follow-through), a marshalling of community resources, and extraordinary doses of support, compassion, and, sometimes, even tough love.

Choose your Battles: When a Child Chooses a Different Path or Is in Crisis

For young adults who choose a different path, few battles are worth fighting. Your main task is to support them when the culture may not. For example, speak proudly of the son who decides to pursue a trade after high school instead of going to college. If necessary, learn more about homosexuality, and defend your gay daughter or son to those who may be ignorant. Don't hide or patronize your child who has a disability. Include him in public events, and let him stretch his abilities. Don't berate a pregnant daughter about her sexual relationship with the father of the baby—that's history. Do talk with her about a lifestyle that will prevent this in the future, and encourage and support the couple—and, whenever possible, defend her to those who misplace judgment.

Perhaps the main issue revolves around household guidelines for the boomerang child who returns home for an undetermined amount of time. This probably isn't as much of a battle if expectations about chores, financial contributions, and keeping each other informed of plans are clear ahead of time. If possible, set a deadline for the extended visit. Remember, your goal is his independence, which may mean eviction if he isn't moving toward self-sufficiency. Certainly, young adults with severe disabilities or illnesses may be an exception to this.

When the child isn't the different one but your relationship is different because you're a stepparent, your reaction and behavior will depend a lot on how long you've been in this role. If it's been so long that this distinction no longer makes any difference, proceed as any good parent would. If there's still some sensitivity or unfinished business about your role with your young adult, the rule is to go slowly.

If you're a stepparent, support your spouse (the biological parent) and confer with the absent biological parent when possible and appropriate. For example, let's say your stepdaughter is getting married. She wants both her father (your husband) and her mother (the ex-wife) to walk her down the aisle. This puts you, the stepmother, in an awkward position and without an escort. If you're on friendly terms with the ex-wife and have enough self-esteem, you might just walk down the aisle alone, or accompanied by another family member. If this doesn't feel comfortable, the bride may walk down the aisle independently, with both sets of parents preceding her and blessing her at the altar. There are other combinations, but the point is not the procession dynamics as much as the process of conferring sensitively with all parties and respecting the important roles that both biological parent and stepparent had in the raising of this young adult. Don't create an unnecessary battle.

If you're in a raw or estranged relationship with a stepchild, this usually means that some disagreement or crisis has blocked the relationship. It may be a matter of letting time heal a rift, but more often,

professional help is needed to break through an unhealthy or dysfunctional family history.

IN CRISIS

For young adults in crisis, the battle may be between when to com-
passionately support them and when to hold them accountable for
continuing to make bad choices. An alcoholic son needs your acceptance but not your compliance. If he's not willing to enter a treatment
program, don't fight with him over it–just don't rescue him by giving
him room and board and covering for him at work. It's not a fight; it's
just following through on previously agreed-upon ground rules you
have already set for your household. You'll always love him, but love
doesn't mean enabling him to continue self-destructive behavior.

. . . . .

IN THEIR OWN WORDS: WHAT PARENTS
LIKE YOU AND YOUNG ADULTS ARE
SAYING ABOUT THIS PERIOD OF
TRANSITION

Special Needs Child
"My twenty-two-year-old son has Downs Syndrome. The
hardest thing for me to learn was that I couldn't fully protect
Adam from making mistakes. As parents we understood that
Adam has the right to "the dignity of risk." We all take risks
every day and Adam should be allowed to face those same
risks. We all learn from our mistakes and so has Adam. I
decided early on that I would have the same high expectations of all three of our children, according to their capabilities." (Cindy S., parent, Naperville, Illinois)

"My wife and I have four children. Our twenty-year-old, Ken, has Asperger's Syndrome. The main thing I've learned is not to make comparisons among our children. The spiritual challenge I've faced is trying to figure out what is care and what is enabling (treating Ken more like a child than needed). I would berate myself saying, 'I ought to be smart enough to say the right thing to help Ken get past an obstacle.' Eventually, I said to him, 'Ken, I love you, but I've done all I can. It's now your responsibility to stay in college.' It may take an extra year, but so far, he's rising to the challenge." (Jim H., parent, Joliet, Illinois)

Tough Love
"Our nineteen-year-old son dropped out of a private college and came home to get his bearings. Eventually he entered a local community college and got a part-time job but he still had a lot of growing up to do. Meanwhile, my husband got a job in another state and we were planning to move. Although our son could have moved with us, the psychologist he was working with recommended that he be forced to take responsibility for his life and get his own apartment. The last thing I did before we moved was to pay his first month's rent and then he would be on his own. It took him seven years to get a two-year degree, but now he has a 3.3 at a four-year college. It's hard for two Type A parents to know how to guide a less driven, less organized child. The counselor gave us the courage to exercise tough love." (Margaret Ann M., parent, St. Louis, Missouri)

Addictions
"I'm a recovering alcoholic. I've been clean now for forty-two years but have been alert to it with our own six children. Indeed, one son became an abuser of both alcohol and

drugs. Our whole family agreed to enter a treatment program. I've learned not to put unnecessary temptation in front of Matt. He used to be in charge of finances for an apartment building we own. My husband and I decided to take back this responsibility. Matt recently told us he was sorry for his behavior and he has been clean for a few months. Stepping back works." (Peg G., parent, San Francisco, California)

Homosexuality

"I am a lesbian. My parents believe that it is a choice that I have made and that it is against God's will for my life. I believe that God made me who I am and smiles on me for being who he made me to be. This has led to a rift between us that affects everything. It took me years to come to grips with who I am and really love myself. They tried for years to 'change' me and sent me to Christian counselors. I now have a life partner, and it is sad to me that my parents cannot accept who I am because I feel like they are missing out on truly being a part of my life." (Krista A., young adult, Cincinnati, Ohio)

Pregnancy

"Working through my own challenge and fear for the welfare of my pregnant-before-marriage daughter better equipped me to later do more meaningful post-abortion ministry. My daughter chose life, but I could reassure other women and men who didn't choose life and never told their parents, that their parents would likely forgive." (Beverly H., parent, Madison, Wisconsin)

"At nineteen I had my first child. At twenty-two I had my second. I'm now twenty-seven, still unmarried and living in a homeless shelter. Could my parents have done anything differently to make my life better? I doubt it, but they did the best they could. My mother had me before she was married, and I was brought up in a very dysfunctional environment. I don't think my parents had the resources to do anything different. Just as I had my children young, so did they. But I've decided the cycle ends with me. It took courage to have my children when I could have terminated the pregnancies, and now that courage is helping me turn my life around. Now I realize I can choose to give my children something better. Although I grew up going to church, I didn't attend from my teen years on, but I do have faith in God and now attend church regularly." (LaKesha G., young adult, Alexandria Virginia)

Divorce

"Divorce is always a loss. There is no way around the grieving for all involved, parents and children alike. While I don't claim that my former spouse and I negotiated our divorce perfectly, I'm proud that we committed ourselves to being respectful and doing what was in the best interest of our two children (ten and six years old at the time). My hope is that the children learned through our divorcing that painful experiences can be negotiated within the context of caring relationships. Because the marriage between their father and I did not work out, it did not mean that their Dad and I did not care about them or that marriage never works. I remarried three years after our divorce. (My former spouse is also remarried.) The children have models of caring, committed married relationships that work. Anna is now a vivacious, self-confident, twenty-four-year-old woman. A lot of that is her natural temperament, but I also think that she learned some of her resilience through the rigors of my former spouse and me negotiating our relationship. There is no way to make divorce less painful, but I think remaining respectful of each other helped our children." (Jo Ann Z., parent, Kalamazoo, Michigan)

"Seldom does a child welcome a parent's divorce, but I remember thinking, even as a child, that it was a good thing that Mom and Dad divorced. I knew from an early age that they were different from other married couples. I always remember Mom and Dad each having their separate time with us kids. I've never thought of my stepfather as a replacement for my father or as a threat. He's my mom's husband. What I see in my mom and stepdad are caring, committed partners in a relationship that works." (Anna S., young adult, Kalamazoo, Michigan)

"My first wife and I were both Catholic but had different styles of expressing our faith. This became a quiet battleground throughout our marriage, and we probably gave mixed messages to our two children, especially during their teen years, about the practice of faith. As our differences were magnified over time, it may or may not have contributed to our young adults' alienation with the institutional church, but it definitely drove a wedge between my wife and me—eventually to the point of our divorce. I know my son and daughter to be fine young adults with values that I'm proud of, but it is a sadness and mystery to me that for all the ways I tried to raise them in faith, that they don't set foot into any church today. (Jack B., parent, Redlands, California)

In Their Own Way, in Their Own Time...
"My son had a difficult time in high school. He suffered from panic attacks and school phobia until his junior year when he was finally expelled due to excessive absences. Fortunately, he had learned enough to pass the GED exam,

but I was still concerned that he would be stigmatized as a dropout and would never be able make a decent living. Since then, he has pursued his passion of hiking and camping in the wilderness. With his AmeriCorps wilderness experience, he qualifies for seasonal work in several state parks. I realize now that as a parent I thought I knew what was best for my son based on the standards for success that were established by society. However, my son had to find his own path. As a result he has been able to succeed on his own terms. I am proud now as I see that he has matured into a strong, independent, and self-assured young man." (Poppy E., parent, Park Hills, Kentucky)

"Sometimes I blame myself that both my sons married unbaptized women. Did I push religion on them as children? Was I not a sufficient example of a Christian mother or spouse? Church has always been a large part of my life, and I took my sons to religious classes, altar boy service, and confirmation prep. Although I encouraged my teens to complete the confirmation programs, both opted not to be confirmed with their classmates. I felt the pangs of silent criticism from family members and fellow parishioners. Was it just easier not to argue and cajole them to be confirmed? Then, about two years ago, the pastoral associate called to ask for my daughter-in-law's phone number saying that she was interested in attending RCIA. She and I had discussed religion and spirituality many times and she knew why I chose to continue to embrace my faith despite frustrations. Last Easter, my daughter-in-law was baptized and confirmed and my younger son was confirmed." (Pat G. parent, Tewksbury, Massachusetts)

QUESTIONS FOR REFLECTION

1. Which virtues seem most relevant to you at this stage of parenting? Consider especially wisdom, unconditional love, and forgiveness. Which comes easiest to you? Which is hardest? Why?
2. Which of this chapter's challenges or stories do you identify with most? How have you tried so far to understand your young adult better?
3. Have you ever sought counseling or joined a support group to help you deal with your feelings about parenting a young adult who marches to the beat of a different drummer or faces special difficulties in life? In what ways did you find the counseling helpful?
4. When do you feel compassion for your young adult and feel compelled to move mountains to protect or help her? Have you ever needed to use "tough love" with her, allowing difficult consequences to take their natural course?
5. Is it hardest for you to forgive others, your young adult, or yourself? What's been the hardest thing you've tried to forgive?

Let Us Pray

For young adults who march to a different drummer, may they find
the beat that gives them fulfillment.
For ourselves as we move ever deeper into surrendering our lives
for the good of others.
We ask forgiveness for our mistakes and
wisdom to know you better.

We pray to the Lord.

Lord, hear our prayer.

: THOUGHTS TO KEEP IN MIND :

Forgive, but verify.

You are responsible for the process in raising your
children, not the outcome.

CONCLUSION

THE BOTTOM LINE

ONE ADVANTAGE OF AGE IS seeing how the pendulum of fashions and ideas swing from one extreme to the other. One year Croc shoes are in; the next they're passé. One decade permissiveness is the parenting mode of choice; the next decade it is debunked and "good old-fashioned discipline" returns among all the parenting gurus. In the world of "church style" things move much more slowly, but still the pendulum seems to swing.

In the early Christian community, there were many expressions of faith while believers tried to figure out how to be faithful to Jesus, who had just left them. Eventually Scripture, rules, and rituals became codified so that there would be more unity. As unity grows, however, flexibility often becomes stifled, and some believers balk at what feels like an overly strict form of religious practice. As the pendulum swings back and forth, those who live in the middle may hit a fortuitous balance between the church tightening its identity and becoming more open and inclusive.

The same is true for books. It's nice if you happen to be living in the age when the pendulum hits middle, but if not, realize that as it moves from side to side people eventually make necessary corrections for the extremes. It just takes a long time for what is old to become new. This book is an attempt to allow the wisdom of age to meet the energy of youth in the middle. If it's not modern enough for you, stick around a while.

When all is said and done, and our young adult children no longer live under our roof, how does a parent deal with regret, disappointment, or even puffed-up pride with how our children turned out? The mantra I repeat to myself is, "I am responsible for the process I used in raising my child, not the outcome."

This helps when, despite conscientiously modeling a healthy lifestyle, ensuring that our children got a thorough religious education, and perhaps shelling out a fair amount of money for schools and lessons, our kids made decisions with which we disagreed. As believers, we believe that God gives us free will. Faith that is forced or superficial does not honor our Creator. Let go, and have confidence that God loves each of our children at least as much as we do. This is faith.

But, what if you've read the above paragraph and say to yourself, "Hmmm, that's fine for those responsible parents who really *did* model their faith, took their kids to church every Sunday, and so forth, but I'm not so sure I'm a stellar example of faithful parenting." The answer here is similar but with an addendum: Remember that God is both a loving *and* forgiving God. We must follow by forgiving ourselves. Even the best of parents makes mistakes, and even the worst of parents can't change history. All we can do is pick ourselves up, dust ourselves off, and start again to be the best person we can be. It's never too late to love again and to forgive ourselves. Then, let go and have confidence that God loves each of our children at least as much as we *want* to.

Appendix A

SURVEY RESULTS

Although I've been a professional family minister for more than thirty years and with my husband raised four young adults, I wanted to ground this book in more than my own observations, academic training, and professional experience. Thus, I invited more than four thousand parents and young adults to answer survey questions, and more than six hundred responded, giving me a sense of what many parents and their young adults struggle with, especially regarding issues of faith.

Although this was not a scientific survey in terms of random sampling, it still reflected a large number of parents and young adults who cared about their faith. Many parents passed the survey on to their own children, some of whom were no longer practicing any organized religion. Some pastoral ministers forwarded it to the young adults with whom they had contact. The number of parents and young adults were roughly equal in both surveys.

Of course, the challenge is in interpreting the data. Faith, in the sense of organized religion, was important to the majority of the parents. Thus, the pool of respondents was primarily people who actively practice a faith, most often Catholics.

I am indebted to the many people who not only completed the surveys but also generously shared their stories of hope and anguish.

Following are the survey questions that had measurable responses:

For parents

Which of the following life transitions has been the most difficult for you as the parent of a young adult? Why?

Your young adult's college years	17.8%
Your young adult's transition to job or career	6.8%
Your young adult's marriage	6.8%
Your young adult's first child (your first grandchild)	1.3%
Your young adult returning to live with you	6.3%
None have been particularly difficult for me	10.9%
Other	12.7%

In regard to your young adult and faith, did you find any of the following issues to be a challenge?

Mass attendance	17.9%
Career choice	1.9%
Cohabitation	12.2%
Interfaith marriage	5.1%
Parenting decisions	3.9%
Consumerism/materialism	8.2%
Prayer/faith practices	9.6%
Behavior/morals	6.5%
My grandchildren are not being raised in my faith	4.2%
Divorce	3.7%
Lifestyle choices	2.5%
Other	3.4%

For young adults:

Which of the following life transitions has been the most difficult for you? Why?

College years	9.4%
Job/Career start-up	21.6%
Marriage	12.2%
First child	9.4%
None have been particularly difficult for me	9.4%
Other	9.4%

Appendix B

A Sending-Forth Blessing

(For parents of young adults leaving home)

As a "DOMESTIC CHURCH," FAMILIES ideally will mark the time when a son or daughter leaves home for college, the military, a year of service, or just to be on their own by having a special "sending off" at home. There comes a time, however, after your young adult has gone into the world, when you're left with the empty place at the table and mixed emotions. The support of a faith community can be healing and hopeful at this time.

I adapted this blessing ritual, created by Laura Baum-Parr of the Family Life Office of the Archdiocese of Omaha, to help parents deal with this life transition for both their young adult and themselves. Ideally, it would be sponsored by the faith community in which the parents worship. Although this prayer service could be done at any time, September would be the time when most parents say their good-byes and are ready to gather in a prayerful setting.

Opening song: "Gather Your People, O Lord"

Opening prayer: "Lord, our God, look with kindness on our sons and daughters whom the faith of the church commends to your tender care. We ask your blessing upon them, so that they may grow in Christian maturity and, by the power of the Holy Spirit, become Christ's witness in the world, revealing your goodness to all they meet. We ask this in your name. Amen."

First reading: A reading from the first book of Corinthians *(Read 1 Corinthians 12:4–11)*

Second reading: A reading from the Acts of the Apostles *(Read Acts 2:1–4)*

Reflection: *(The prayer leader highlights the reality that each of our young adults has unique gifts to offer the broader human family.)* Just as the apostles and disciples were sent out at Pentecost, we parents now send our sons and daughters out to the world. We may no longer be physically present to them, but we trust that the same Spirit that filled the early church with courage and wisdom will be with our own sons and daughters in the years ahead.

LITANY OF THE GIFTS OF THE HOLY SPIRIT
Response: "Send us your spirit, O Lord."

Holy Spirit, grant our children your gift of wisdom so that they may know that all life comes from you and, therefore, is sacred. *Response.*

Holy Spirit, grant our children your gift of understanding so that they may see and accept themselves as they are. *Response.*

Holy Spirit, grant our children your gift of counsel so that they may seek out help from others, especially when they are in need. *Response.*

Holy Spirit, grant our children your gift of fortitude so that they may have the courage to do what is right and just. *Response.*

Holy Spirit, grant our children your gift of knowledge so that they may have a burning desire to seek the truth. *Response.*

Holy Spirit, grant our children your gift of piety so that their relationship with God will be awakened. *Response.*

Holy Spirit, grant our children your gift of fear of the Lord so that they may forever keep alive their awareness of your awesome, gentle presence in their lives. *Response.*

Holy Spirit, we ask you to give us the wisdom and courage to help our sons and daughters become the persons you desire them to be. *Response.*

Holy Spirit, help us to discover how to fill this new empty space in our lives in such a way that brings us peace and deepens our trust in you. *Response.*

SHARING QUESTIONS

What do you think is your young adult's best gift, quality, or talent?

What empty space is in your life now that your son or daughter has left home? How might that space become sacred space?

PRAYER RITUAL WITH INCENSE

Prepare a bed of coals outside (as in a barbecue grill). Give each participant a few grains of incense to sprinkle on the coals. This will cause a fragrant smoke to rise.

Reflection (Prayer leader): "Our prayers rise to you, O Lord, like incense. Just as the incense rises and disappears, so to our sons and daughters have risen and left our presence–for a time. Fill our hearts not with fear but hope for their future and ours."

Closing prayer (All): "Loving God, may we always give witness to the power of your Spirit, and never stop encouraging our sons and daughters to become the persons you desire them to be. Protect and watch over them that they may connect with goodness all around them, possess the gift of your peace, and be a light to this world. Thank you for sending forth your Spirit to be with us at all times. Thank you for leading us out of the confines of our sorrows and fears and into the wide expansiveness of your love. Amen."

Closing song: "City of God"

Books

Garber, Steven. *The Fabric of Faithfulness: Weaving Together Belief and Behavior*. Downers Grove, Ill: InterVarsity, 2007.

Hakenewerth, Quentin, S.M. *Growing in the Virtues of Jesus*. Dayton, Ohio: North American Center for Marianist Studies (NACMS), 2004.

Hayes, Mike. *Googling God: The Religious Landscape of People in Their 20s and 30s*. New York: Paulist, 2007.

Kaye, Kenneth, with Nick Kaye. *Trust Me. Helping Our Young Adults Financially*. New York: iUniverse, 2009.

Kelly, Matthew. *The Rhythm of Life: Living Every Day with Passion and Purpose*. New York: Fireside, 2004.

———. *Building Better Families: A Practical Guide to Raising Amazing Children*. New York: Ballantine, 2008.

McKinney, Mary Benet, O.S.B. *Sharing Wisdom: A Process for Group Decision Making*. Valencia, Calif.: Tabor, 1987.

Nemzoff, Ruth, *Don't Bite Your Tongue: How to Foster Rewarding Relationships with Your Adult Children*. New York: Palgrave Macmillan, 2008.

Chesto, Kathleen O'Connell. *Exploring the New Family: Parents and their Young Adults in Transition*. Winona, Minn.: Saint Mary's Press, 2001.

———. *Family Prayer for Family Times*. Mystic, Ct.: Twenty-Third Publications, 1995.

Popenoe, David, and Barbara Dafoe Whitehead. *The State of Our Unions: Sex Without Strings, Relationships Without Rings*. The National Marriage Project, 2000. Available at http://moralis-sues.hp.infoseek.co.jp/mi/NMPAR2000.pdf.

———. "Should We Live Together?" The National Marriage Project, 2000. www.virginia.edu/marriageproject/pdfs/swlt2.pdf.

Rolheiser, Ronald. *The Holy Longing: The Search for a Christian Spirituality*. New York: Doubleday, 1999.

Rohr, Richard. *Contemplation in Action*. Chestnut Ridge, N.Y.: Crossroad, 2006.

Smith, Christian, and Melina Lundquist Denton. *Soul Searching: The Religious and Spiritual Lives of American Teenagers*. New York: Oxford University Press, 2009.

Smith, Christian, and Patricia Snell. *Souls in Transition: The Religious and Spiritual Lives of Emerging Adults*. New York: Oxford University Press, 2009.

Van Epp, John. *How to Avoid Falling in Love with a Jerk*. New York: McGraw-Hill, 2008.

Vogt, Susan. *Raising Kids Who Will Make a Difference: Helping Your Family Live with Integrity, Value Simplicity, and Care for Others*. Chicago: Loyola, 2002.

Marriage Programs and Resources

Family Matters (www.SusanVogt.net)

Marriage, parenting, and spirituality articles and resources for couples and parents, including *Marriage Moments* and *Parenting Pointers,* which are free brief weekly e-mails of wisdom to support marriage and parents.

Arusi Network (www.arusi.org)

Marriage and social support for African-American Christian marriages.

Founders: Andrew and Terri Lyke, Lyke to Lyke Consultants

Chicago, Illinois

312-751-8264

Association for Couples in Marriage Enrichment (www.better-marriages.org)

ACME is an international nonprofit, nonsectarian organization that provides enrichment opportunities and resources to strengthen couple relationships and enhance personal growth, mutual fulfillment, and family wellness.

Winston-Salem, North Carolina

800-634-8325 or 336-724-1526

E-mail: acme@bettermarriages.org

Couple Communication (www.couplecommunication.com)

Couples learn eleven interpersonal skills for effective talking and listening, plus processes for better decision making, conflict resolution, and anger management.

Sherod Miller, PH.D., codeveloper

Interpersonal Communication Programs, Inc.

Evergreen, Colorado

800-328-5099

E-mail: icp@comskills.com

For Your Marriage (www.ForYourMarriage.org)

A website sponsored by the United States Conference of Catholic Bishops that includes various articles, resources, quizzes, and background information about how to have a healthy marriage.

National Marriage Encounter (www.marriage-encounter.org)

NME promotes and encourages marriage and family life by offering Marriage Encounter weekends and a support community. It's open to couples of all faiths as well as those with no religious affiliation.

Chuck and Sandy Ogg, NME Business Administrators

4704 Jamerson Place

Orlando, Florida 32807

800-828-3351

E-Mail: emory78@comcast.net

National Marriage Project (www.virginia.edu/marriageproject)

The NMP originally was based at Rutgers University but moved to the University of Virginia in 2009. Its mission is to provide research and analysis on the state of marriage in America and to educate the public on the social, economic, and cultural conditions affecting marital success and child well-being.

Renovacion Conyugal (www.wwme.org)

A Spanish-speaking marriage enrichment weekend program to help couples strengthen their marriage. It also helps troubled marriages where separation or divorce is a possibility or has already occurred.

Family Life Office

Diocese of Orlando, Florida

407-246-4882

Worldwide Marriage Encounter (www.wwme.org)

WWME is a weekend experience that teaches a technique of loving communication to promote intimate and responsible relationships and offers community support for the sacramental lifestyle modeled by the presenters. Offered in English, Spanish, and Korean.

2210 East Highland Avenue #106

San Bernardino, California 92404

909-863-9963

E-Mail: office@wwme.org

Retrouvaille (www.retrouvaille.org)

Retrouvaille is a weekend experience combined with a series of six to twelve post weekend sessions over three months. The emphasis of the program is on communication in marriage between husband and wife. There are neither group dynamics nor group discussion on the weekend.

800-470-2230

The Third Option (www.thethirdoption.com)

The Third Option is an ongoing group program for marriages. It combines fourteen unique skill-building workshops, sharing by mentor couples who have overcome marital problems, and a support group component. Because it uses a "self-change" model, one spouse may come alone.

Pat Ennis

315-472-6754, x320

E-mail: pat@thethirdoption.com

Beyond Affairs Network (www.beyondaffairs.com)

BAN is an international support group with local chapters for people recovering from the devastating experience of a spouse's affair.

Anne and Brian Brecht

604-859-9393

E-mail: anne@passionatelife.ca

Parenting Resources

Christian Family Movement (www.cfm.org)

CFM is a network of families supporting each other in living their faith in daily life at home, in the workplace, and in their communities. Resource booklets are published each year to facilitate meetings.

Paul and Missy Parkinson, executive directors

812-962-5508

E-mail: office@cfm.org

Family Wellness Associates Survival Skills for Healthy Families

FLASH is a unique twelve-hour parenting education program that involves the whole family and teaches practical, lifelong skills that strengthen and empower marriages and families.

George Doub, M.F.C.C., M.Div., Ana Morante, L.M.F.T., and Erin Simile, L.M.F.T.

Scotts Valley, California
831-440-0279
E-mail:families@familywellness.com

Retreat and Prayer Resources
Center for Action and Contemplation (www.cacradicalgrace.org)
Founded by Fr. Richard Rohr, O.S.F., CAC is a center for experiential education, encouraging the transformation of human consciousness through contemplation, equipping people to be instruments of peaceful change in the world.
P.O. Box 12464,
Albuquerque, New Mexico 87195
505-242-9588
Couple Prayer Series (www.coupleprayer.org)
A six-week series to help married and engaged couples develop closer relationships with God and each other as they learn to pray in safe, close, and comfortable ways.
Deacon Bob and Kathy Ovies
P.O. Box 1270
Royal Oak, Michigan 48068
248-546-7253
host@coupleprayer.org

Young Adult Resources
Busted Halo (www.bustedhalo.com)
This online magazine for spiritual seekers has various interesting articles and features, including a national "Church Search," which lists parishes recommended by young adults for a welcoming spirit, good homilies, good music, and community.

ABOUT THE AUTHOR

Susan V. Vogt is an award-winning freelance writer and speaker on marriage, parenting, and spirituality. A professional Catholic family minister for over thirty years, she has served as an adviser to the U.S. Conference of Catholic Bishops' Committee on Marriage and Family. She lives in Covington, Kentucky, with her husband, Jim. Their four young adult children wander the world in search of love and meaning, and try to make our planet a better place for all. Sometimes they are successful, sometimes not. She blogs about simplifying one's life at www.susanvogt.net/blog.